108 G+1 HOUSE PLAN DESIGNS

WITH VASTU SHASTRA TIPS

A S SETHUPATHI

ISBN 978-93-5458-561-6

Published in India 2021 by Pencil

A brand of
One Point Six Technologies Pvt. Ltd.
123, Building J2, Shram Seva Premises,
Wadala Truck Terminal, Wadala (E)
Mumbai 400037, Maharashtra, INDIA
E connect@thepencilapp.com
W www.thepencilapp.com

Author biography

AS SETHUPATHI is from Anthiyur, Erode district, Tamilnadu, India. He studied BE Civil Engineering (2013) and M tech Structural Engineering (2015) at the Hindustan University, Chennai. He's the founder of the www.houseplansdaily.com website. He learned Vastu Shastra by himself. Also, he learned to make House plans as per Vastu Shastra. He makes blueprints, Interior and Exterior design drawings in both 2D and 3D, Section plans, Elevation Drawings, Structural, Electrical, and Plumbing Drawings. After some research, he came to know many people in this world searching for House plan ideas to build their dream house. So he planned to make House Plan books as per Vastu Shastra for the people who need house plans. He hopes this book will be more helpful for people Searching for house plan ideas. Also, this book is useful for Civil Engineers, Architects, Civil, Architecture, and Interior Design Students. He sincerely thanks you for buying this book. If this book is helpful for you kindly refer to your friends and also give a review of this book. Thank you.

CONTENTS

About the Book

108 G+1 House plan Designs as per vastu Shastra Book. It contains 108 various land areas of beautiful House Plans. This Book covers the home plan design of East, West, North, and South Directions. There are 27 Different land sizes of house plans that are featured in each direction. This book contains 484 sqft to 2400 sqft House Plans. These plans are suitable for any plot, also you can use these plans for your reference too. In this Book, the available house plans land areas are 22x22 484 sqft, 20x30 600sqft, 30x20 600 sqft, 25x25 625 sqft, 26x26 676 sqft, 20x40 800 sqft, 22x40 880 sqft, 18x50 900 sqft, 30x30 900 sqft, 26x36 936 sqft, 36x26 936 sqft, 24x40 960 sqft, 26x40 1040 sqft, 33x33 1089 sqft, 23x50 1150 sqft, 20x60 1200 sqft, 30x40 1200 sqft, 40x30 1200 sqft, 25x50 1250 sqft, 27x50 1350 sqft, 35x40 1400 sqft,30x50 1500 sqft, 30x60 1800 sqft, 36x50 1800 sqft, 45x45 2025 sqft, 40x60 2400 sqft, 60x40 2400 sqft. These home plans are created as per vastu Shastra principles. This House plan book is very useful for the people who searching for house plans to build their Dream house, Civil, structural engineers, architects, civil, Architecture, and Interior Design Students. They can keep this book as a reference too. Civil Engineers and Architects can show these plans to their clients as sample house plans. Also, by using this book they can design the best vastu plans. Many varieties of

G+1 House plan ideas are given in this book. In these home plans, pillars are placed in the size 1'6"x9". Items of Furniture like sofa, Beds, Tv, Toilet, Stove, the washbasin is placed as per vastu. Moreover, the details of where to place Bore well, Underground water tanks, and Septic tanks are mentioned in some house plans. I hope this book will be more helpful for people all over the world. For more House Plans check out the website www.houseplansdaily.com. Thank You.

Dedication

I dedicate this book to all the people in this world.
My special thanks to
The Universe
God
My parents

Vastu Shastra Mantra

Bhoomi Putraya Dheemahi
Om Anugraha Roopaya Vidhmahe
Tanno Vastu Purusha Prachodayat.

EAST FACING HOUSE PLANS

22X22 484 SQFT EAST FACING HOUSE PLAN

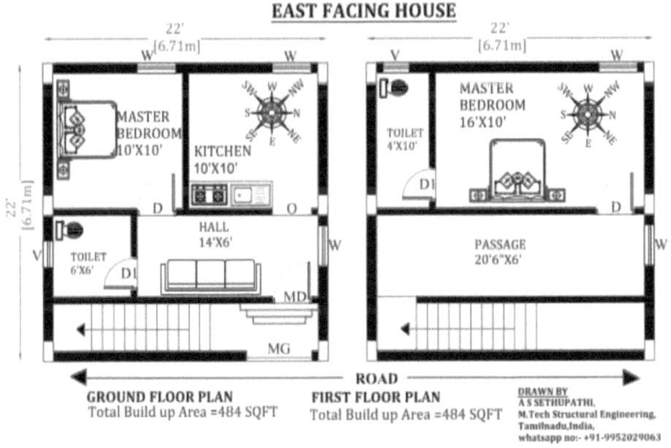

22x22 484 sqft East facing G+1 Tiny House Plan is shown in the above image. In the ground floor plan, the kitchen is in the northwest direction. The Master Bedroom is placed in the southwest direction. Hall is in the Northeast direction. Common toilet is available in the southeast direction. In the First floor plan, one Master bedroom with an attached toilet and the passage is available. The staircase is available in the southeast direction outside of the house. Pillars are marked in this small home plan in the size of 1'6"x9".This home design plan is useful for people who searching for small house plan ideas.

30X20 600 SQFT EAST FACING HOUSE PLAN

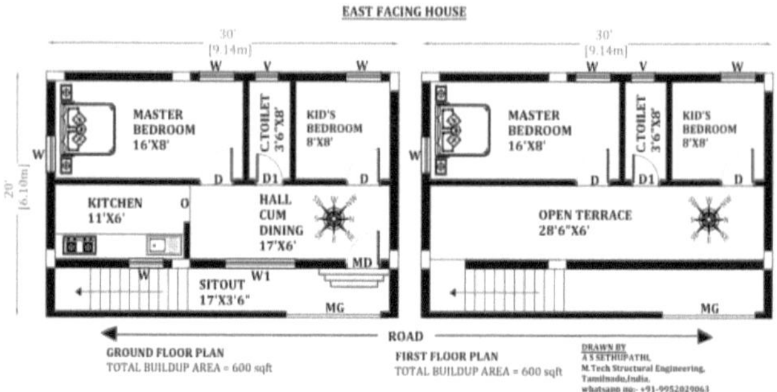

30x20 600 sqft East facing G+1 small House Plan is shown in the above image. In the ground floor plan, the kitchen is in the southeast direction. The Master Bedroom is placed in the southwest direction. Kid's or the children's bedroom is kept in the northwest direction of the house. The common toilet is placed in the west direction. Hall cum Dining is in the Northeast direction. Sitout is available outside of the house is in the northeast direction.

On the First floor plan, The Master Bedroom is placed in the southwest direction. The kid's bedroom is kept in the northwest direction. The common toilet is placed in the west direction. The open terrace is in the east. The Staircase is placed in the southeast direction. Pillars are mentioned in this home plan in the size of 1'6"x9".This house design plan is useful for people who searching for tiny house plan ideas.

20X30 600 SQFT EAST FACING HOUSE PLAN

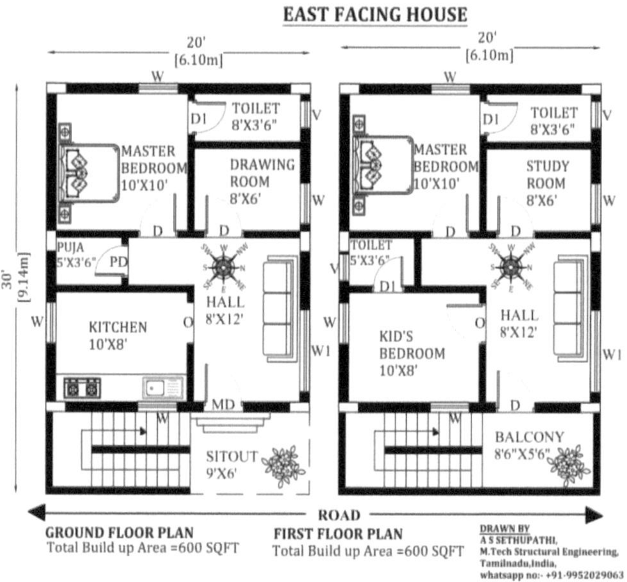

20x30 600 sqft East facing Home plan Furniture Design is given in this image. In this G+1 house design plan, On the ground floor, the kitchen is placed in the southeast direction of the home. Puja room is available in between the kitchen and the master bedroom is in the south direction. The Hall or the living room is in the northeast direction. The Master bedroom is placed in the southwest direction with an attached toilet is in the northwest. The drawing room is placed in the north. Finally sitout is available outside of the house in the northeast direction.

On the First floor plan, The Master bedroom is placed in the southwest direction with an attached toilet is in the northwest. The study room is placed in the north. And the Kid's bedroom is placed in the southwest direction with an attached toilet is in the south. Hall is in the northeast direction. Moreover, the balcony is available in the northeast direction. The Staircase is placed outside of the house in the southeast direction. Furniture is set in this drawing as per the vastu shastra principle. Columns are marked in this home plan and its size is 1'6"x9".

25X25 625 SQFT EAST FACING HOUSE PLAN

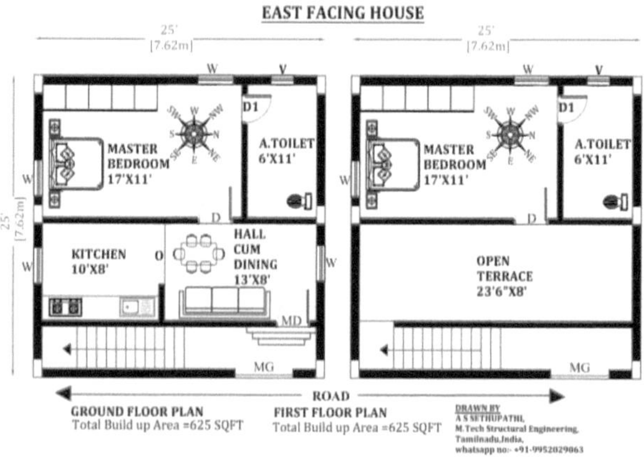

25x25 625 sqft East facing G+1 Home Plan is shown in the above image. In the ground floor plan, the kitchen is kept in the southeast direction. The Master Bedroom is placed in the southwest direction. An attached toilet is available in the northwest. Hall cum dining is in the Northeast direction.

On the First floor plan, one Master bedroom with an attached toilet and an open terrace is available. The staircase is available in the southeast direction outside of the house. Pillars are placed in this home plan in the size of 1'6"x9".This home design plan is useful for people who searching for home plan ideas.

26X26 676 SQFT EAST FACING HOUSE PLAN

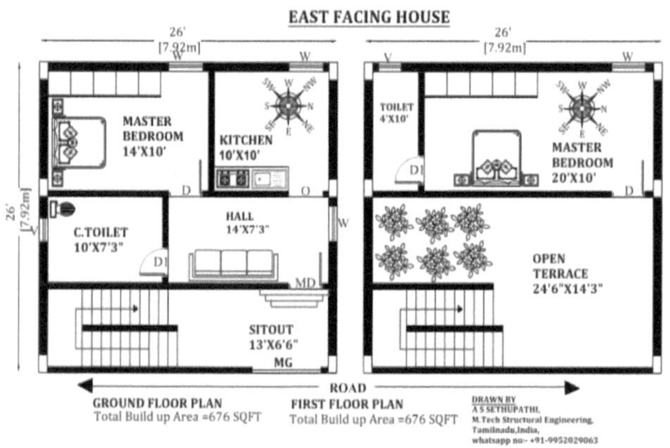

26x26 676 sqft East facing House Plan is shown in the above image. On the ground floor plan, the kitchen is in the northwest direction. As per Vastu Shastra making a kitchen in the northwest direction is the second option. The Master Bedroom is placed in the southwest direction. Hall is in the Northeast direction. Common toilet is available in the south direction. Sitout is available in the northeast direction.

On the First floor plan, the Bedroom is available in the

northwest with an attached toilet is in the southwest. Also, an open terrace is available. The staircase is available in the southeast direction outside of the house. The size of the pillar is 1'6"x9" which is marked in this plan.

20X40 800 SQFT EAST FACING HOUSE PLAN

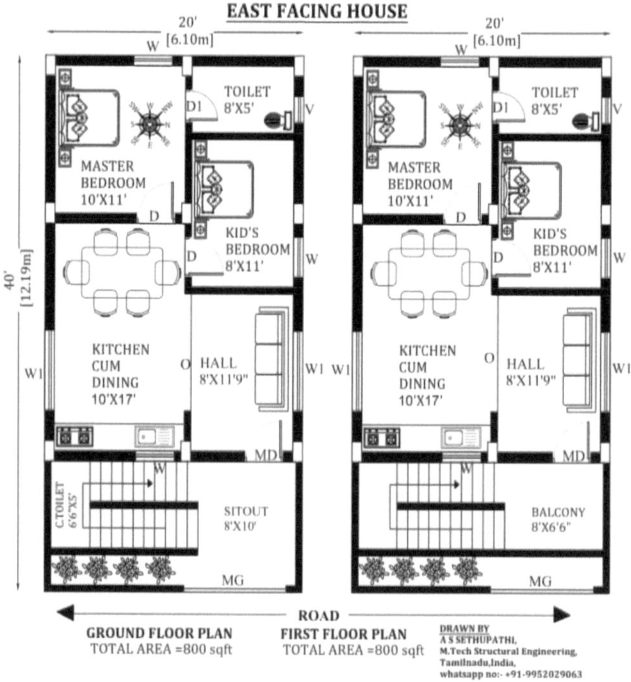

20x40 800 sqft East facing Home plan with Furniture Design is given in this image. Most commonly East facing houses are More auspicious as per vastu Shastra. In this

G+1 home design ground floor plan, the kitchen cum dining is placed in the southeast direction. The Master bedroom is set in the southwest direction with an attached toilet is in the northwest. Kid's Bedroom is in the north direction. The Hall or the living room is in the northeast direction. The sitout is available outside of the house in the northeast direction.

The First-floor plan is also the same as the Ground floor, the kitchen cum dining is placed in the southeast direction. The Master bedroom is placed in the southwest direction with an attached toilet is in the northwest. The kid's bedroom is placed in the north direction. The Hall or the living room is in the northeast direction. Moreover, the balcony is available in the northeast direction. The Staircase is situated outside of the house in the southeast direction. Furniture is set in this drawing as per the vastu shastra. Columns are mentioned in this house plan and its size is 1'6"x9".

22X40 880 SQFT EAST FACING HOUSE PLAN

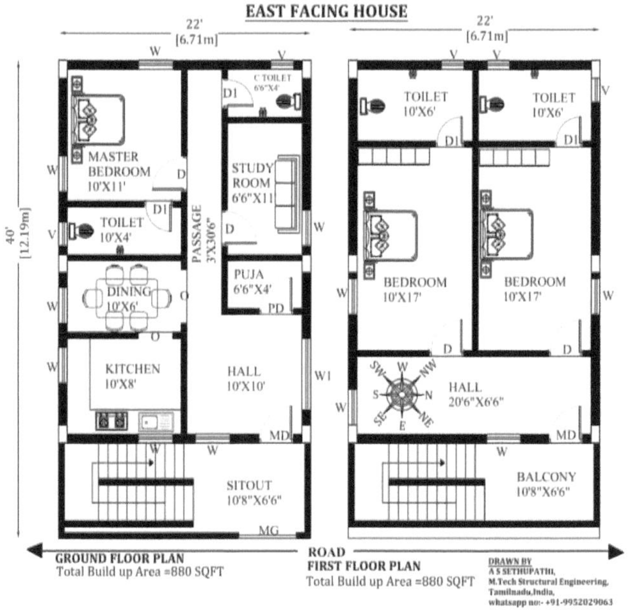

22x40 880 sqft East facing Home plan Design with furniture is given in this image. In this G+1 house design plan, On the ground floor, the kitchen is placed in the southeast direction of the home. Dining near the kitchen is in the south direction. Puja room is available in the north direction. The Hall or the living room is available in the northeast direction. The Master bedroom is placed in the southwest direction with an attached toilet is in the south. The study room is placed in the north. Common toilet is placed in the northwest. Finally, the sitout is placed outside of the house in the northeast direction.

On the First floor plan, there are two bedrooms. The first bedroom is placed in the south direction with an attached toilet is in the southwest. The second bedroom is placed in the north direction with an attached toilet is in the northwest. Hall is in the east direction. Moreover, the balcony is available in the northeast direction. The Staircase is placed outside of the house in the southeast direction. Furniture is set in this drawing as per the vastu. Columns are marked in this house plan and its size is 1’6”x9”.

18X50 900 SQFT EAST FACING HOUSE PLAN

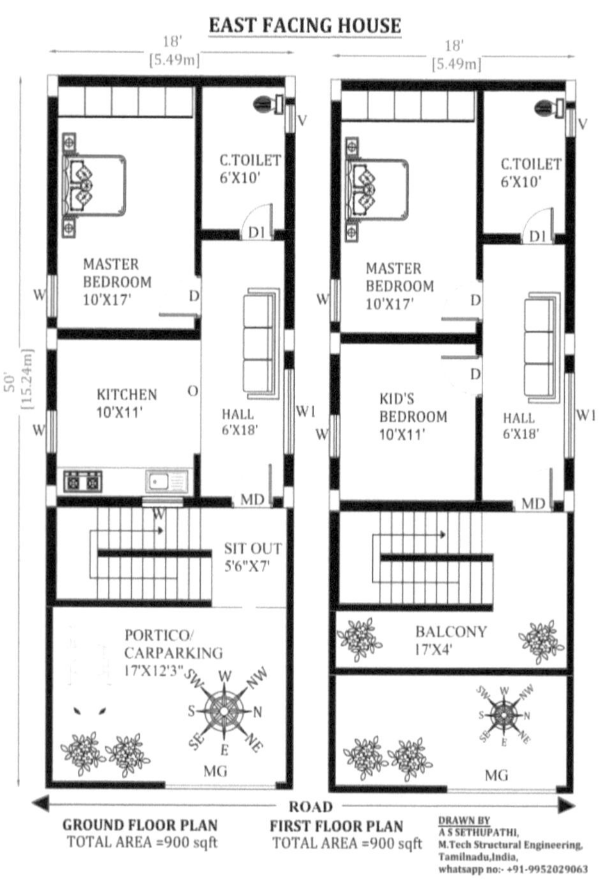

18x50 900 sqft East facing House plan is given in this image. In this G+1 house design plan, On the ground floor, the kitchen is placed in the southeast direction. The Hall is in the northeast direction. The Master bedroom is placed in the southwest direction. The Common toilet is available in the northwest. The sitout is placed outside of the house in the northeast direction. Moreover, Portico or the car parking is in the East direction.

On the First floor plan, The Master bedroom is placed in the southwest direction. The Kid's bedroom is placed in the south direction. The Common toilet is available in the northwest. Hall is in the northeast direction. The balcony is available in the northeast direction. The Staircase is placed outside of the house in the southeast direction. Pillars are placed in this home plan and its size is 1'6"x9".

30X30 900 SQFT EAST FACING HOUSE PLAN

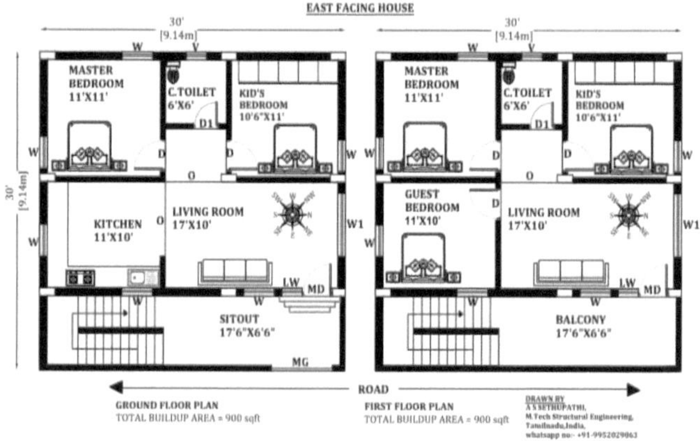

30x30 900 sqft East facing Home plan is given in this image. In this G+1 home design plan, On the ground floor, the kitchen is placed in the southeast direction. The living room is available in the northeast direction. The Master bedroom is placed in the southwest direction. The Common toilet is available in the west. The kid's bedroom is kept in the northwest direction. While sleeping keep your head in the east or south direction is so good as per vastu. The sitout is placed outside of the house in the northeast direction.

On the First floor plan, The Master bedroom is placed in the southwest direction. The Kid's bedroom is placed in the northwest direction. The guest bedroom is placed in the southeast direction. The Common toilet is available in the west. The living room is in the northeast direction. The balcony is available in the northeast direction. The Staircase is placed outside of the house in the southeast direction. Pillars are placed in this plan and its size is 1'6"x9".

26X36 936 SQFT EAST FACING HOUSE PLAN

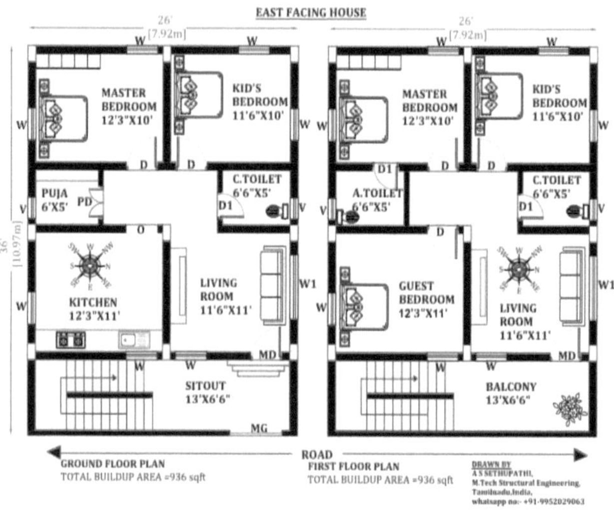

26x36 936 sqft East facing House plan is given in this image. In this G+1 house design plan, On the ground floor, the kitchen is placed in the southeast direction. While cooking the person wanna stand facing east direction according to vastu shastra. The living room is available in the northeast direction. The Puja room is available in between the kitchen room and the master bedroom is in the south direction. The Master bedroom is placed in the southwest direction. The kid's bedroom is kept in the northwest direction. The Common toilet is available in the north. The sitout is placed outside of the house in the northeast direction.

On the First floor plan, there are three bedrooms. The Master bedroom is placed in the southwest direction with an attached toilet is in the south direction. The Kid's bedroom is placed in the northwest direction. The guest bedroom is placed in the southeast direction. The Common toilet is available in the north. The living room is in the northeast direction. The balcony is available in the northeast direction. The Staircase is placed outside of the house in the southeast direction. Pillars are placed in this house plan and its size is 1'6"x9".

36X26 936 SQFT EAST FACING HOUSE PLAN

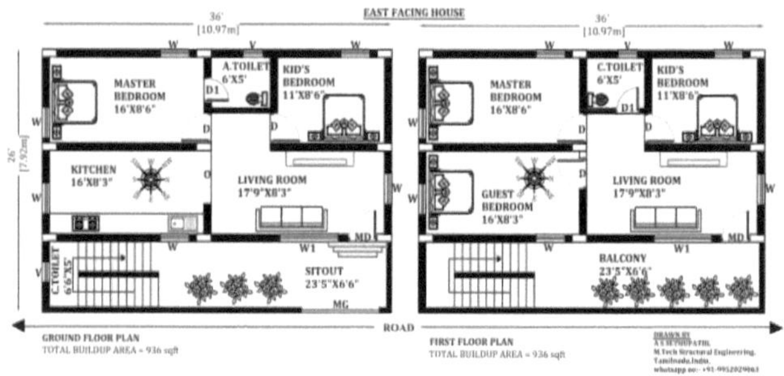

36x26 936 sqft East facing House plan is given in this image. In this G+1 house plan, On the ground floor, the kitchen is placed in the southeast direction. The living room is available in the northeast direction. The Master bedroom is placed in the southwest direction with an attached toilet is in the west. The kid's bedroom is kept in the northwest direction. The Common toilet is available in the southeast under the staircase. The sitout is available outside of the house in the northeast direction.

On the First floor plan, there are 3 bedrooms. The Master bedroom is in the southwest direction. The Kid's bedroom is placed in the northwest direction. The guest bedroom is placed in the southeast direction. The Common toilet is available in the west. The living room is available in the northeast direction. The balcony is placed in the northeast direction. The Staircase is placed outside of the house in the southeast direction. Pillars are mentioned in this house plan.

24X40 960 SQFT EAST FACING HOUSE PLAN

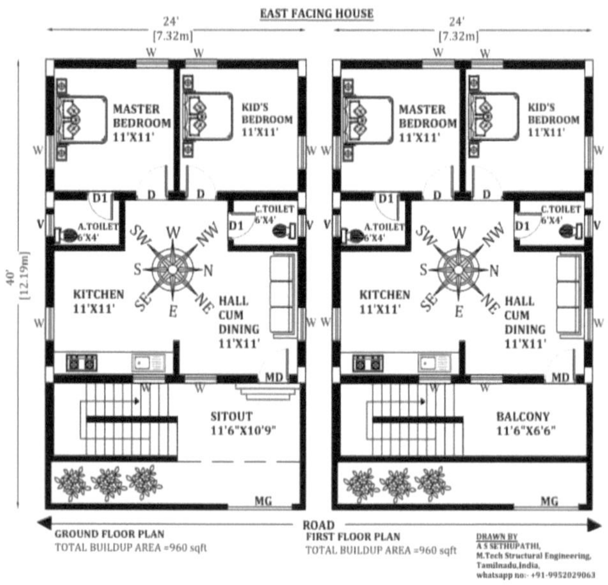

24x40 960 sqft East facing House design plan is given in this image. In this G+1 house design plan, On the ground floor, the kitchen is placed in the southeast direction. The hall cum Dining is available in the northeast direction. The Master bedroom is placed in the southwest direction with an attached toilet is in the south. The kid's bedroom is kept in the northwest direction. The Common toilet is available in the north. The sitout is placed outside of the house in the northeast direction.

The first floor also the same as the ground floor plan. In which, the kitchen is in the southeast direction. The hall cum Dining is available in the northeast direction. The Master bedroom is kept in the southwest direction with an attached toilet is in the south. The kid's bedroom is placed in the northwest direction. The Common toilet is available in the north. The balcony is placed outside of the house in the northeast direction. Pillars are marked in this plan perfectly.

26X40 1040 SQFT EAST FACING HOUSE PLAN

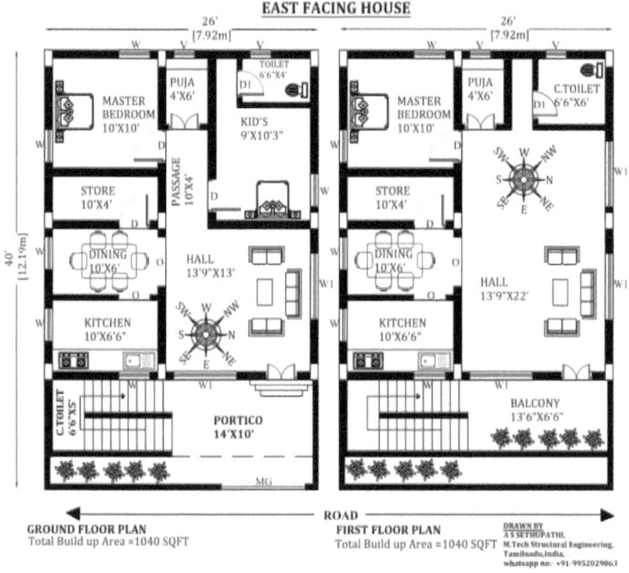

26x40 1040 sqft East facing Home plan Design with beautiful furniture is given in this image. In this G+1 home design plan, On the ground floor, the kitchen is placed in the southeast direction of the home. Dining near the kitchen is in the south direction. The store room near the dining is in the south. Puja room is available in the west direction. The Hall or the living room is available in the northeast direction. The Master bedroom is placed in the southwest direction. The kid's bedroom is placed in the north with an attached toilet is in the northwest. Common toilet is placed in the southeast under the stairs. Finally, the portico is placed outside of the house in the northeast direction.

On the First floor plan, the kitchen is placed in the southeast direction of the home. Dining near the kitchen is in the south direction. The store room near the dining is in the south. Puja room is available in the west direction. The Hall or the living room is available in the northeast direction. The Master bedroom is placed in the southwest direction. Common toilet is placed in the northwest direction. The balcony is placed outside of the house in the northeast direction.
The Staircase is placed outside of the house in the southeast direction. The items of furniture are placed in this home plan drawing as per the vastu. Moreover, the pillars are mentioned in this house plan and their size is 1’6”x9”.

33X33 1089 SQFT EAST FACING HOUSE PLAN

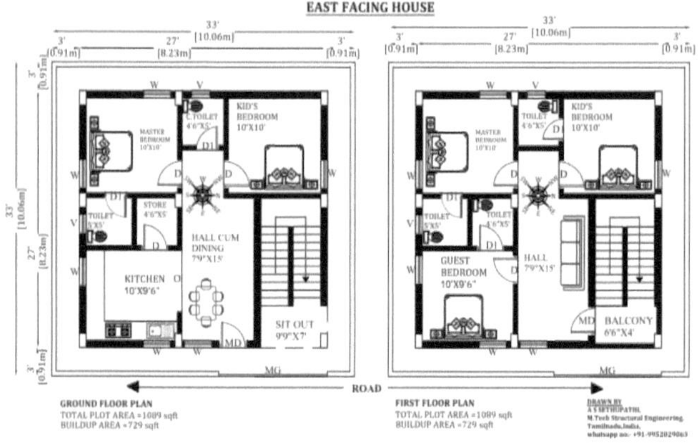

33x33 1089 sqft East facing House plan is given in this image. On the ground floor plan, the kitchen is placed in the southeast direction. The hall cum dining is available in the northeast direction. The storeroom is placed near the kitchen. The Master bedroom is placed in the southwest direction with an attached toilet is in the south. The kid's bedroom is kept in the northwest direction. The Common toilet is available in the west. The sitout is available outside of the house in the northeast direction.

On the First floor plan, there are three bedrooms with an attached toilet. The Master bedroom is in the southwest direction with an attached toilet is in the south. The Kid's bedroom is placed in the northwest direction with an attached toilet is in the west. The guest bedroom is placed in the southeast direction with an attached toilet is in the south. The hall or living room is available in the northeast direction. The balcony is placed in the northeast direction. The Staircase is placed outside of the house in the north direction. Pillars are mentioned in this house plan. The setback is given in all four directions.

23X50 1150 SQFT EAST FACING HOUSE PLAN

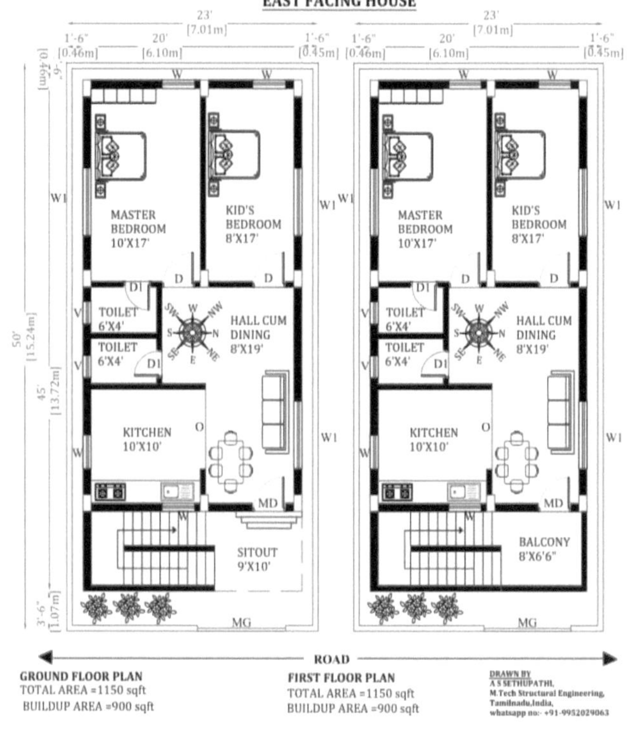

23x50 1150 sqft East facing House design plan is given in this image. In this G+1 house design plan, On the ground floor, the kitchen is placed in the southeast direction. The hall cum Dining is available in the northeast direction. The Master bedroom is placed in the southwest direction with an attached toilet is in the south. The kid's bedroom is kept in the northwest direction. The Common toilet is available in the south. The sitout is placed outside of the house in the northeast direction.

The First floor also the same as the Ground floor plan. In that, the kitchen is in the southeast direction. The hall cum Dining is available in the northeast direction. The Master bedroom is kept in the southwest direction with an attached toilet is in the south. The kid's bedroom is placed in the northwest direction. The Common toilet is available in the south. The balcony is placed outside of the house in the northeast direction. The setback is given in all four directions. Pillars are marked in this home plan exactly.

20X60 1200 SQFT EAST FACING HOUSE PLAN

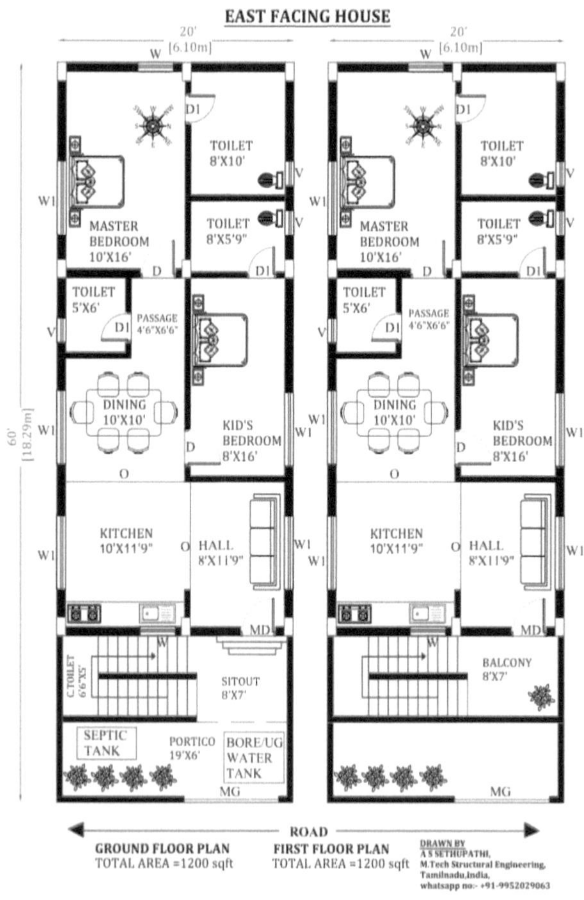

20x60 1200 sqft East facing House design plan is given in this image. In this G+1 home plan, On the ground floor, the kitchen is placed in the southeast direction. Dining near the kitchen is in the south direction. The hall is available in the northeast direction. The Master bedroom is placed in the southwest direction with an attached toilet is in the northwest. The kid's bedroom is placed in the north direction with an attached toilet is in the north. The Common toilet is available in the south. One more common toilet is placed outside of the house under the stairs is in the south. The sitout is placed outside of the house in the northeast direction. Septic tank is mentioned in this plan, it is available in the southeast direction. And Borewell or the underground water tank is placed in the northeast direction.

The First floor also the same as the Ground floor plan. In that, the kitchen is placed in the southeast direction. Dining near the kitchen is in the south direction. The hall is available in the northeast direction. The Master bedroom is placed in the southwest direction with an attached toilet is in the northwest. The kid's bedroom is placed in the north direction with an attached toilet is in the north. The Common toilet is available in the south. The balcony is placed outside of the house in the northeast. Pillars are marked in this home plan are in the size 1'6"x9". The staircase is placed in the south near the kitchen outside of the house.

30X40 1200 SQFT EAST FACING HOUSE PLAN

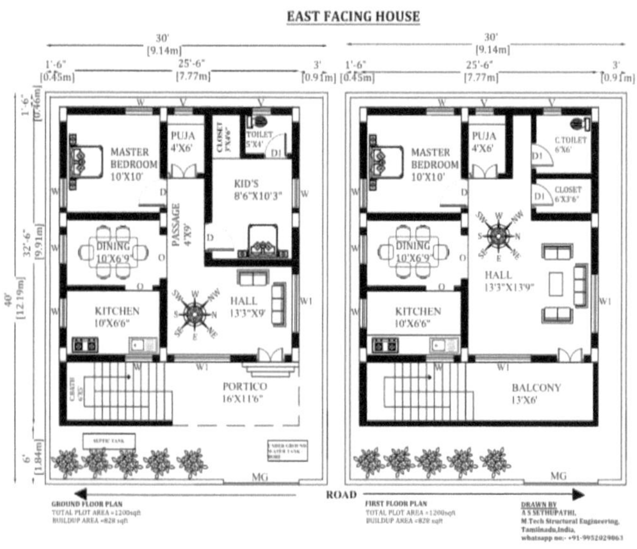

30x40 1200 sqft East facing G+1House plan Design with furniture is given in this image. On the ground floor, the kitchen is placed in the southeast direction of the house. Dining near the kitchen is in the south direction. Puja room is available in the west direction. The Hall or the living room is available in the northeast direction. The Master bedroom is placed in the southwest direction. The kid's bedroom is placed in the north with an attached toilet is in the northwest. Common toilet is placed in the southeast under the stairs. And the portico is placed outside of the house in the northeast direction. In this plan, a septic tank and borewell or underground water tank place details are given as per vastu. The Septic tank is placed in the southeast direction. And Borewell or the underground water tank is placed in the northeast direction.

On the First floor plan, the kitchen is placed in the southeast direction of the house. Dining near the kitchen is in the south direction. Puja room is available in the west direction. The Hall is available in the northeast direction. The Master bedroom is placed in the southwest direction. A common toilet with a closet is available in the northwest direction. The balcony is placed outside of the house in the northeast direction. The Staircase is placed outside of the house in the southeast direction. The set of Furniture is placed in this house plan drawing as per the vastu. Also, the pillars are mentioned in this house plan and their size is 1'6"x9".

40X30 1200 SQFT EAST FACING HOUSE PLAN

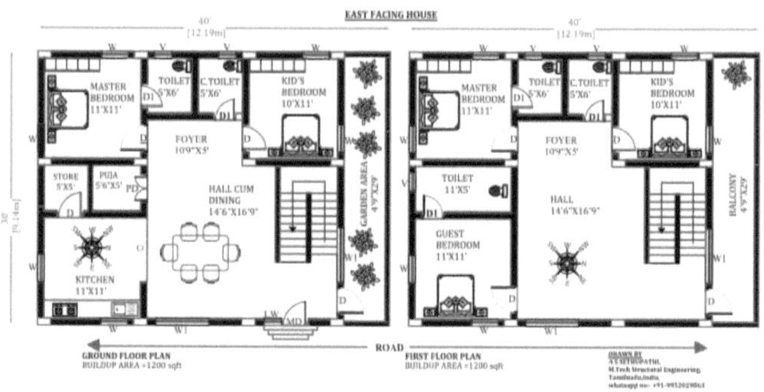

40x30 1200 sqft East facing duplex Home plan is given in this above image. On the ground floor plan, the kitchen is placed in the southeast direction. The hall cum dining is available in the northeast direction. Storeroom is placed near the kitchen is in the south direction. Puja room is placed near the store room is in the south. The Master bedroom is placed in the southwest direction with an attached toilet is in the west. The kid's bedroom is kept in the northwest direction. The Common toilet is available in the west. The Garden area is placed on the north side of the house.

On the First floor plan, there are three bedrooms. The

Master bedroom is in the southwest direction with an attached toilet is in the west. The Kid's bedroom is placed in the northwest direction. The guest bedroom is placed in the southeast direction with an attached toilet is in the south. The Common toilet is placed in the west. The hall or living room is available in the northeast direction. The balcony is placed in the north direction. The Staircase is placed inside of the house in the north direction. Pillars are mentioned in this house plan.

25X50 1250 SQFT EAST FACING HOUSE PLAN

25x50 1250 sqft G+1 East facing House plan with furniture is given in this image. On the ground floor, the kitchen is placed in the southeast direction of the house.

Dining near the kitchen is in the south direction. Puja room is available in the north direction. The Hall or the living room is available in the northeast direction. The Master bedroom is placed in the southwest direction with an attached toilet is in the west. The kid's bedroom is placed in the northwest. Sitout is placed outside of the house in the northeast direction. The place details of the Septic tank are given in this plan, it is placed in the southeast direction. Borewell or the underground water tank is placed in the northeast direction.

On the First floor plan, there are two bedrooms with an attached toilet and a home theatre is available. The Master bedroom is placed in the southwest direction with an attached toilet is in the west. Another bedroom is placed in the north direction with an attached toilet is in the northwest. The Home theatre room is available in the southeast direction. Hall is in the northeast direction. Moreover, the balcony is available in the northeast direction. The Staircase is placed outside of the house in the southeast direction. Pillars are marked in this house plan and their size is 1'6"x9". Dimensions are given clearly in this house plan.

27X50 1350 SQFT EAST FACING HOUSE PLAN

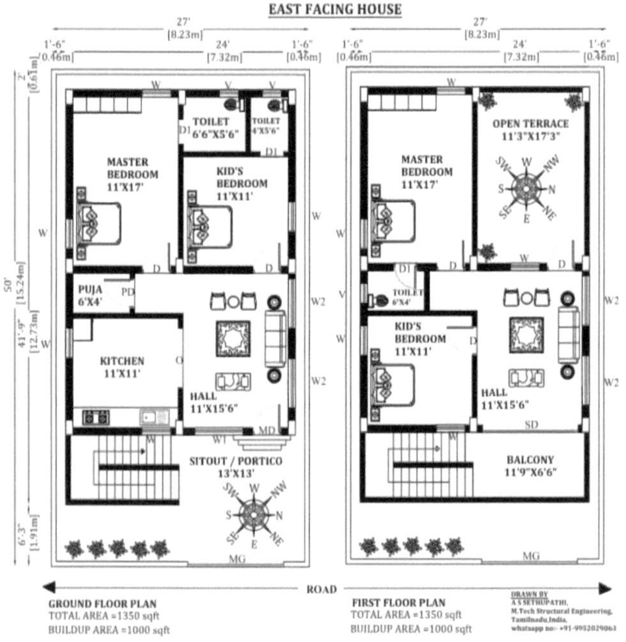

27x50 1350 sqft G+1 East facing House plan is given in this image. On the ground floor, the kitchen is placed in the southeast direction. Puja room is available in the south direction. The Hall is available in the northeast direction. The Master bedroom is placed in the southwest direction with an attached toilet is in the west. The kid's bedroom is placed in the north with an attached toilet is in the northwest. Sitout or the portico is placed outside of the house in the northeast direction.

On the First floor plan, there are two bedrooms. The Master bedroom is placed in the southwest direction with an attached toilet is in the south. The kid's bedroom is placed in the southeast direction. Hall is in the northeast direction. The balcony is available in the northeast direction. The open terrace is placed in the northwest. The Staircase is placed outside of the home in the southeast direction. Pillars are marked in this home plan and their size is 1'6"x9". Room Dimensions are given clearly in this home plan.

35X40 1400 SQFT EAST FACING HOUSE PLAN

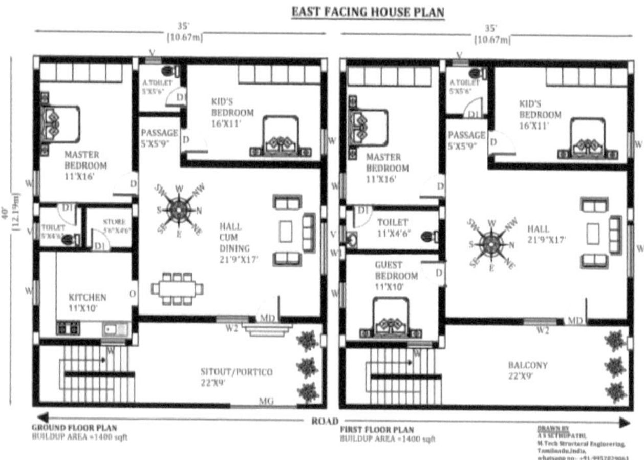

35x40 1400 sqft East facing G+1 Home plan is given in this above image. On the ground floor plan, the kitchen is placed in the southeast direction. The hall cum dining is available in the northeast direction. The storeroom is placed near the kitchen is in the south direction. The Master bedroom is placed in the southwest direction with an attached toilet is in the south. The kid's bedroom is kept in the northwest direction with an attached toilet is in the west. Sitout or portico is placed in the northeast.

On the First floor plan, there are three bedrooms. The Master bedroom is in the southwest direction with an attached toilet is in the south. The Kid's bedroom is placed in the northwest direction. The guest bedroom is placed in the southeast direction. The Common toilet is placed in the west. The hall or living room is available in the northeast direction. The balcony is placed in the northeast direction. The Staircase is placed outside of the house in the southeast direction. Pillars are mentioned clearly in this home plan.

30X50 1500 SQFT EAST FACING HOUSE PLAN

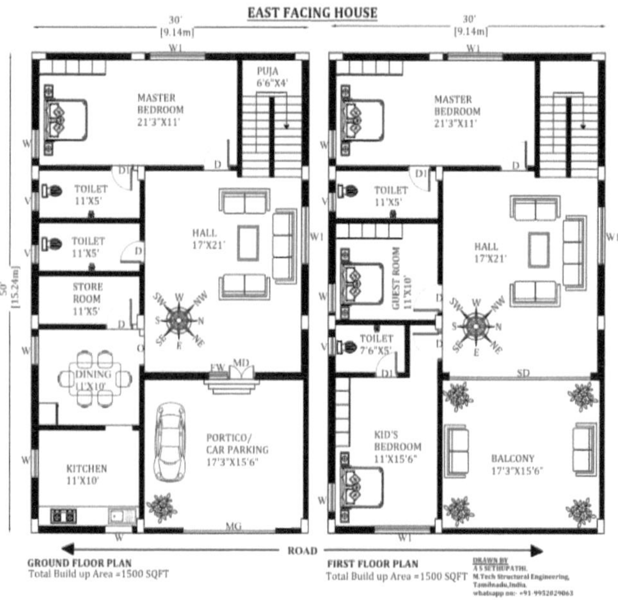

30x50 1500 sqft East facing duplex Home design plan is given in this image. In this G+1 home plan, On the ground floor, the kitchen is placed in the southeast direction. Dining near the kitchen is in the south direction. The storeroom is placed near the dining is in the south.

The hall is available in the northeast direction. The Master bedroom is placed in the southwest direction with an attached toilet is in the south. The Common toilet is available in the south. Puja room is available under the stairs is in the northwest. Portico or the car parking is placed outside of the house in the northeast direction.

On the First floor, The hall is available in the north direction. The Master bedroom is placed in the southwest direction with an attached toilet is in the south. The kid's bedroom is placed in the southeast direction with an attached toilet is in the south. The Guest bedroom is placed in the south. The balcony is placed outside of the house in the northeast. Pillars are marked in this house plan is in the size 1'6"x9".The staircase is placed inside the house in the northwest direction.

30X60 1800 SQFT EAST FACING HOUSE PLAN

30x60 1800 sqft G+1 East facing duplex House design plan is given in this image. On the ground floor, the kitchen is placed in the southeast direction. Dining near the kitchen is in the south direction. The storeroom is placed near the dining is in the south. The hall is available in the north direction. The Master bedroom is placed in the southwest direction with an attached toilet is in the south. The Common toilet is available in the south. Puja room is available under the stairs is in the northwest. Portico or the car parking is placed outside of the house in the northeast direction. The details of the Septic tank are given in this plan, it is placed in the southeast direction. Borewell or the underground water tank is placed in the northeast direction.

On the First floor, The hall or living room is available in the north direction. The Master bedroom is placed in the southwest direction with an attached toilet is in the south. The kid's bedroom is placed in the southeast direction with an attached toilet is in the south. The Home theatre room is placed in the south. The balcony is placed outside of the house in the northeast. Pillars are marked in this home plan are in the size 1'6"x9".The staircase is placed inside the house in the northwest direction of the house.

36X50 1800 SQFT EAST FACING HOUSE PLAN

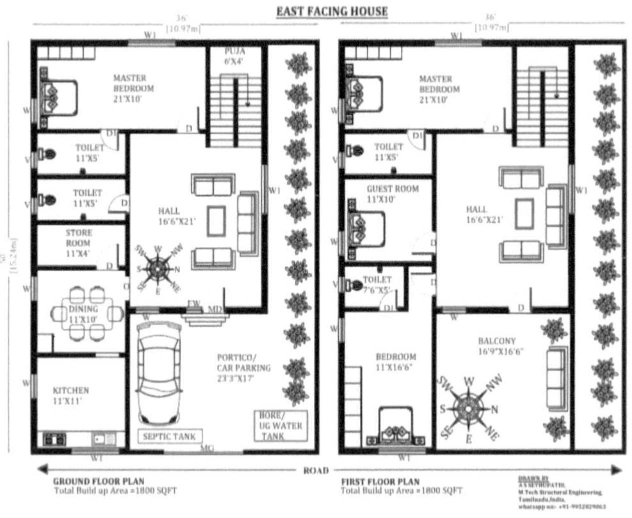

36x50 1800 sqft G+1 East facing duplex Home design plan is given in this image. On the ground floor, the kitchen is placed in the southeast direction. Dining near the kitchen is in the south direction. The storeroom is placed near the dining is in the south. The Master bedroom is placed in the southwest direction with an attached toilet is in the south. The Common toilet is available in the south. Puja room is available under the stairs is in the northwest. The hall is available in the north direction. A portico or car parking is placed outside of the house in the northeast direction. The details of the Septic tank are given in this plan, it is placed in the southeast direction. Borewell or the underground water tank is placed in the northeast direction. The Garden area is available in the north.

On the First floor, The hall or living room is available in the north direction. The Master bedroom is placed in the southwest direction with an attached toilet is in the south. The kid's bedroom is kept in the southeast direction with an attached toilet is in the south. The guest bedroom is placed in the south. The balcony is placed outside of the house in the northeast. The staircase is placed inside the house in the northwest direction of the house.

45X45 2025 SQFT EAST FACING HOUSE PLAN

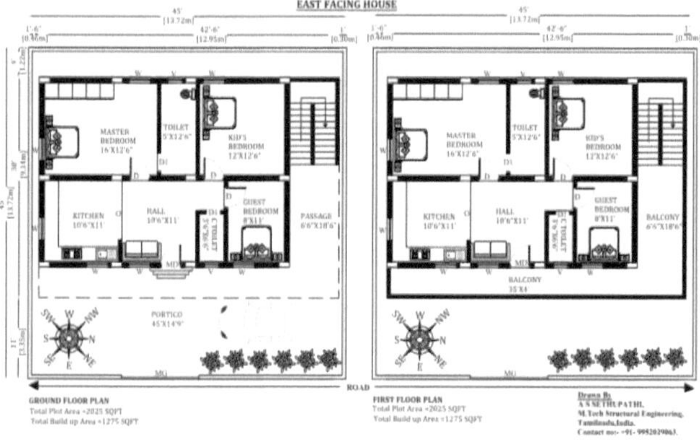

45x45 2025 sqft G+1 East facing House plan is given in this image. On the ground floor plan, the kitchen is placed in the southeast direction of the house. The Hall or the living room is available in the east direction. The Master bedroom is placed in the southwest direction with an attached toilet is in the west. The kid'sid's bedroom is placed in the northwest. The guest bedroom is available in the northeast. Common toilet is placed in the east. Portico and the car parking is placed outside of the house in the east direction. In this plan you can keep the septic tank is in the southeast direction. Also,, you can place Borewell or an underground water tank in the northeast direction.

The firstirst floor plan also the the same as the Ground floor. In that, the kitchen is placed in the southeast direction of the house. The Hall or the living room is available in the east direction. The Master bedroom is placed in the southwest direction with an attached toilet is in the west. The kid's bedroom is placed in the northwest. The guest bedroom is available in the northeast. Common toilet is placed in the east. The balcony is available on the north and east side. Finally, the staircase is placed in the northwest direction.

40X60 2400 SQFT EAST FACING HOUSE PLAN

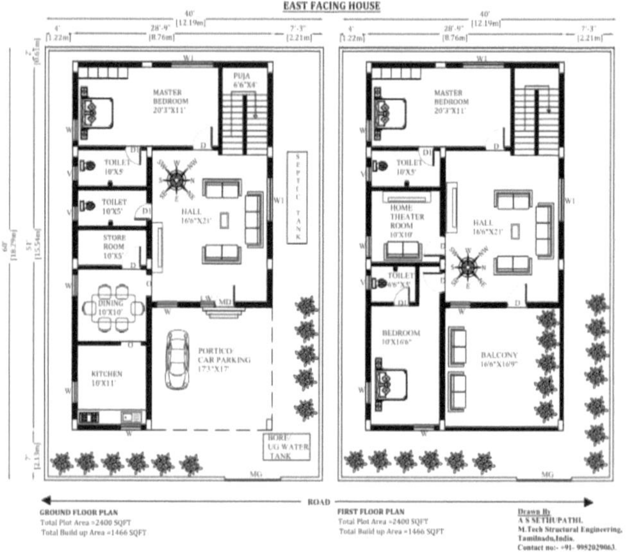

40x60 2400 sqft G+1 East facing duplex House design is given in this image. On the ground floor, the kitchen is placed in the southeast direction. Dining near the kitchen is in the south direction. The storeroom is placed near the dining is in the south. The Master bedroom is placed in the southwest direction with an attached toilet is in the south.

The Common toilet is available in the south. Puja room is available under the stairs is in the northwest. The hall is available in the north direction. A portico or car parking is placed outside of the house in the northeast direction. The details of the Septic tank are given in this plan, it is placed in the northwest direction. Borewell or the underground water tank is placed in the northeast direction. The Garden area is available in the north and east direction.

On the First floor, The hall or living room is available in the north direction. The Master bedroom is placed in the southwest direction with an attached toilet is in the south. The kid's bedroom is placed in the southeast direction with an attached toilet is in the south. Home Theatre room is placed in the south. The balcony is placed outside of the house in the northeast. The staircase is placed inside the house in the northwest direction of the house. Pillars are marked in this home plan are in the size 1'6"x9". Setbacks are given clearly in all four directions. Also, Room dimensions are given perfectly.

60X40 2400 SQFT EAST FACING HOUSE PLAN

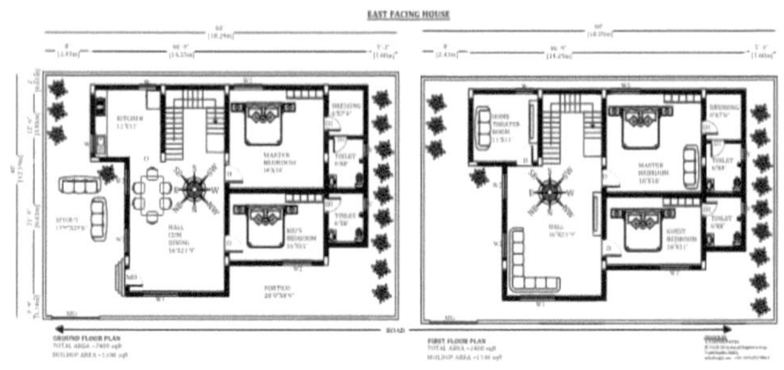

60x40 2400 sqft G+1 East facing House plan is given in this image. On the ground floor plan, the kitchen is placed in the southeast direction of the house. The Hall or the living room is available in the northeast direction. The Master bedroom is placed in the south direction with an attached toilet and the dressing room is in the southwest. The kid's bedroom is placed in the north with an attached toilet is in the northwest. Portico is available in the north direction and the sitout is placed in the east. In this plan you can keep the septic tank is in the northwest direction. And you can place Borewell or an underground water tank in the northeast direction.

On the First floor plan, Hall or the living room is available in the northeast direction. The Master bedroom is placed in the south direction with an attached toilet and the dressing room is in the southwest. The kid's bedroom is placed in the north with an attached toilet is in the northwest. Moreover, the staircase is placed inside of the house is in the south direction. The columns are marked in this plan perfectly.

WEST FACING HOUSE PLANS

22X22 484 SQFT WEST FACING HOUSE PLAN

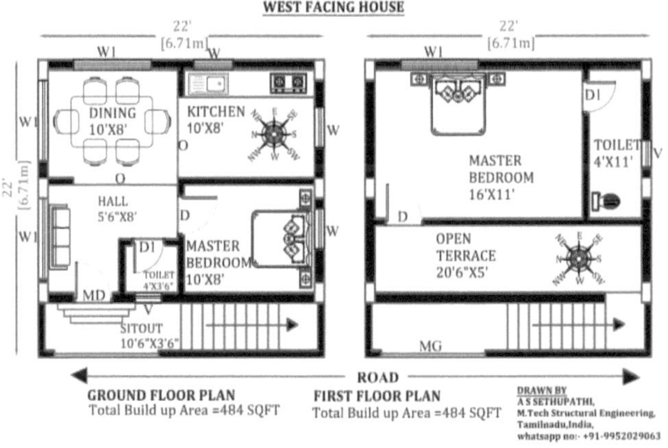

22x22 484 sqft west-facing G+1 small House Plan is shown in the above image. On the ground floor plan, the kitchen is in the southeast direction. Dining near the kitchen is placed in the northeast direction. The Master Bedroom is placed in the southwest direction. Hall is in the Northwest direction. Common toilet is available in the west direction. Sitout is in the northwest direction outside of the house.

On the First floor plan, the Master bedroom is in the

northeast direction with an attached toilet is available in the southeast. The open terrace is in the west direction. The staircase is available in the southwest direction outside of the house. Pillars are marked in this tiny home plan in the size of 1'6"x9".This home design plan is useful for people who looking for tiny house plan ideas.

20X30 600 SQFT WEST FACING HOUSE PLAN

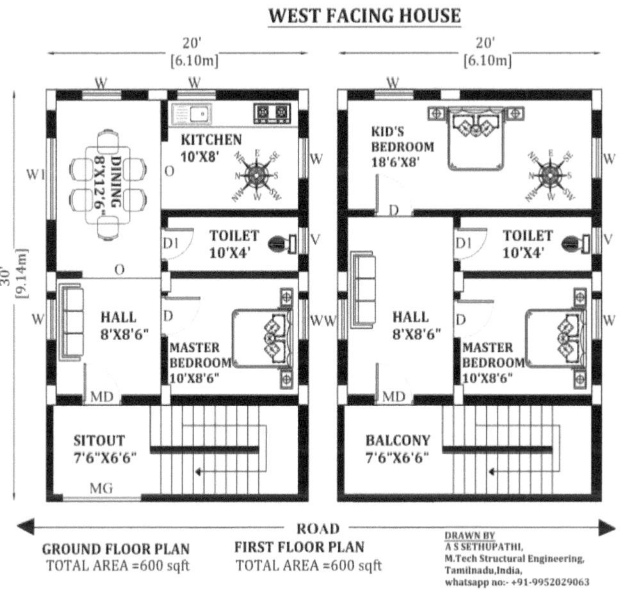

20x30 600 sqft west-facing G+1 House design plan is given in the above image. On the ground floor, the kitchen is placed in the southeast direction. The dining room is in the northeast direction. The living room or the hall is placed in the northwest. Common toilet is placed near the kitchen is in the south. The Master bedroom is placed in the southwest direction. A portico or sitout is placed in the northwest direction outside of the house.

On the First floor plan, The hall or living room is available in the northwest. The Master bedroom is placed in the southwest direction. The kid's bedroom is placed in the east direction. Common toilet is available in the south direction. The staircase is placed outside of the house in the southwest direction. A balcony is available in the northwest direction. The columns are mentioned in this house design are in the size 1'6"x9".Perfect Room dimensions are given in this home floor plan.

30X20 600 SQFT WEST FACING HOUSE PLAN

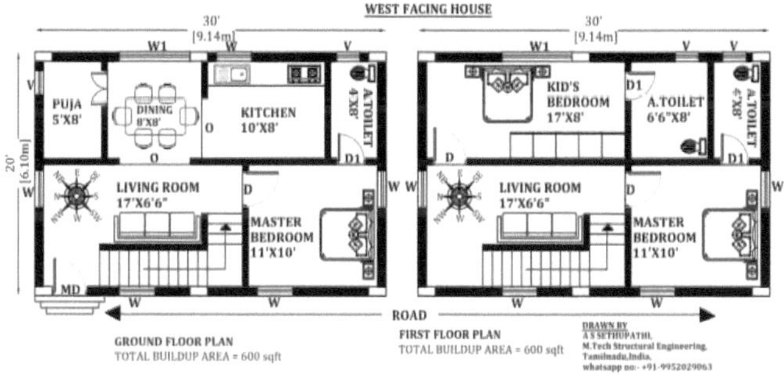

30x20 600 sqft west-facing House design G+1 plan is given in the above image. On the ground floor, the kitchen is placed in the east direction. The dining room is placed near the kitchen is in the east direction. Puja room is kept in the northeast direction of the house. The living room or the hall is placed in the northeast. The Master bedroom is placed in the southwest direction with an attached toilet is in the southeast direction.

On the First floor plan, The hall or living room is available in the northeast. The Master bedroom is placed in the southwest direction with an attached toilet is in the southeast direction. The kid's bedroom is placed in the northeast direction with an attached toilet is in the east.

The staircase is placed inside of the house in the west direction. The pillars are mentioned in this house design are in the size 1'6"x9". Room dimensions are given in this home floor plan very neatly.

25X25 625 SQFT WEST FACING HOUSE PLAN

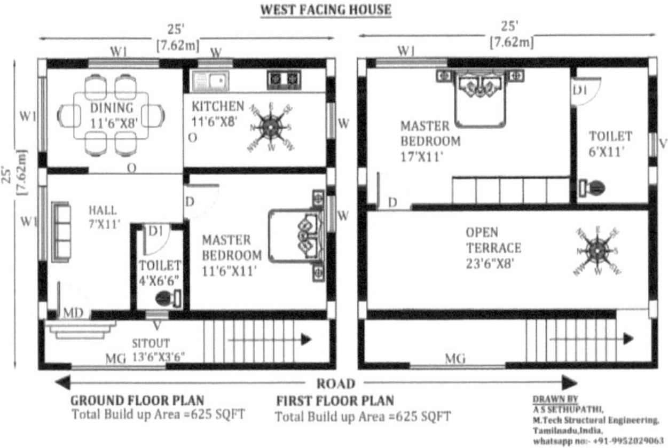

25x25 625 sqft west-facing G+1 tiny House Plan is shown in the above image. On the ground floor plan, the kitchen is in the southeast direction. Dining near the kitchen is placed in the northeast direction. The Master Bedroom is placed in the southwest direction. Hall is in the Northwest direction. Common toilet is available in the west direction. Sitout is in the northwest direction outside of the house.

On the First floor plan, the Master bedroom is in the northeast direction with an attached toilet is available in the southeast. The open terrace is in the west direction.

The staircase is available in the southwest direction outside of the house. Pillars are marked in this tiny house plan in the size of 1'6"x9".This house plan design is very useful for people who looking for tiny house plan ideas.

26X26 676 SQFT WEST FACING HOUSE PLAN

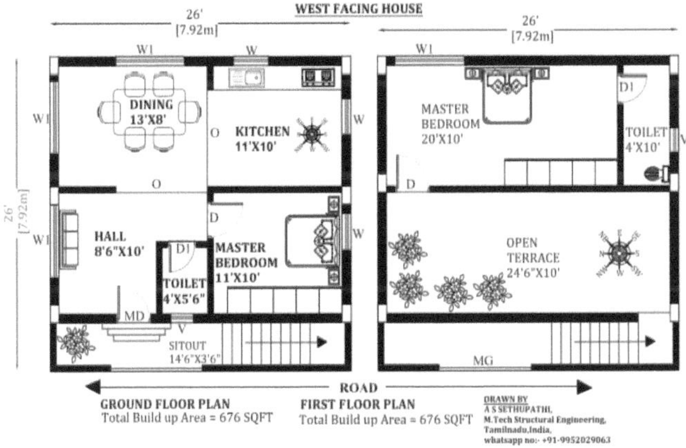

26x26 676 sqft west-facing G+1 small Home Plan is shown in the above image. On the ground floor plan, the kitchen is in the southeast direction. Dining near the kitchen is placed in the northeast direction. The Master Bedroom is placed in the southwest direction. Hall is in the Northwest direction. Common toilet is available in the west direction. Sitout is in the northwest direction outside of the house.

On the First floor plan, the Master bedroom is in the northeast direction with an attached toilet is available in the southeast. The open terrace is in the west direction. The staircase is placed in the southwest direction outside of the house. Pillars are mentioned in this tiny home plan are in the size of 1'6"x9". Furniture are placed in this house plan drawing very nicely.

20X40 800 SQFT WEST FACING HOUSE PLAN

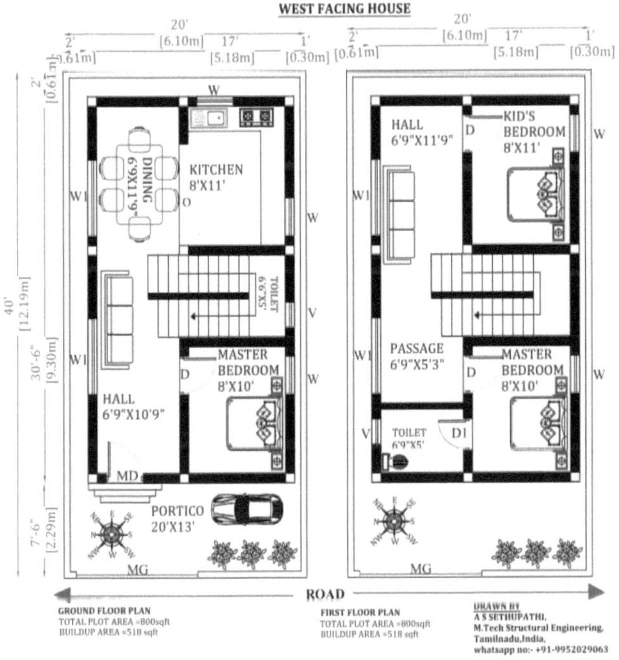

20x40 800 sqft west-facing G+1 House design plan is given in the above image. On the ground floor, the kitchen is placed in the southeast direction. The dining room is in the northeast direction. The living room or the hall is placed in the northwest. Common toilet is placed in the south under the stairs. The Master bedroom is placed in the southwest direction. Portico or sitout is placed in the west direction outside of the house.

On the First floor plan, The hall or living room is available in the northeast. The Master bedroom is placed in the southwest direction with an attached toilet is in the northwest. The kid's bedroom is placed in the southeast direction. The passage is available near the master bedroom. The staircase is placed inside of the house in the south direction. The columns are marked in this house design are in the size 1'6"x9".Perfect Room dimensions are given in this house floor plan.

22X40 880 SQFT WEST FACING HOUSE PLAN

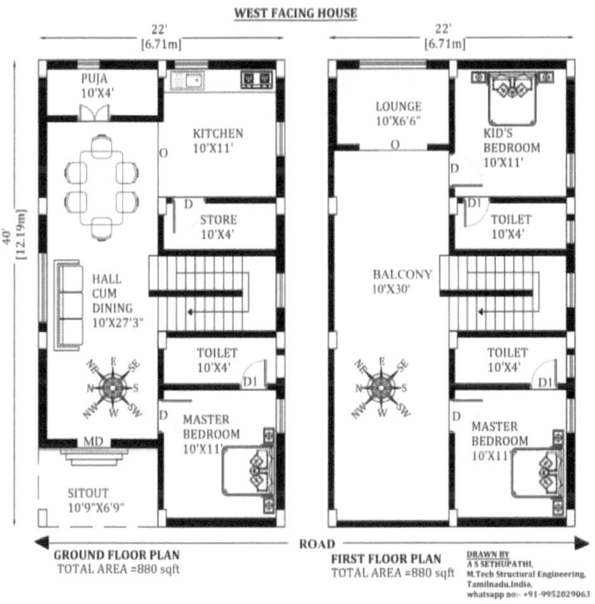

22x40 880 sqft west-facing G+1 House design plan is given in the above image. On the ground floor, the kitchen is placed in the southeast direction. The storeroom is placed near the kitchen is in the south. Hall cum Dining room is placed in the northwest direction. Pooja's room is kept in the northeast. The Master bedroom is placed in the southwest direction with an attached toilet is in the south. A portico or sitout is placed in the northwest direction outside of the house.

On the First floor plan, The Balcony is available in the north. The Master bedroom is placed in the southwest direction with an attached toilet is in the south. The kid's bedroom is placed in the southeast direction with an attached toilet is in the south. The lounge is placed in the northeast direction. The staircase is placed inside of the house in the south direction. The columns are marked in this house design are in the size 1'6"x9".Clear Room dimensions are given in this house floor plan.

18X50 900 SQFT WEST FACING HOUSE PLAN

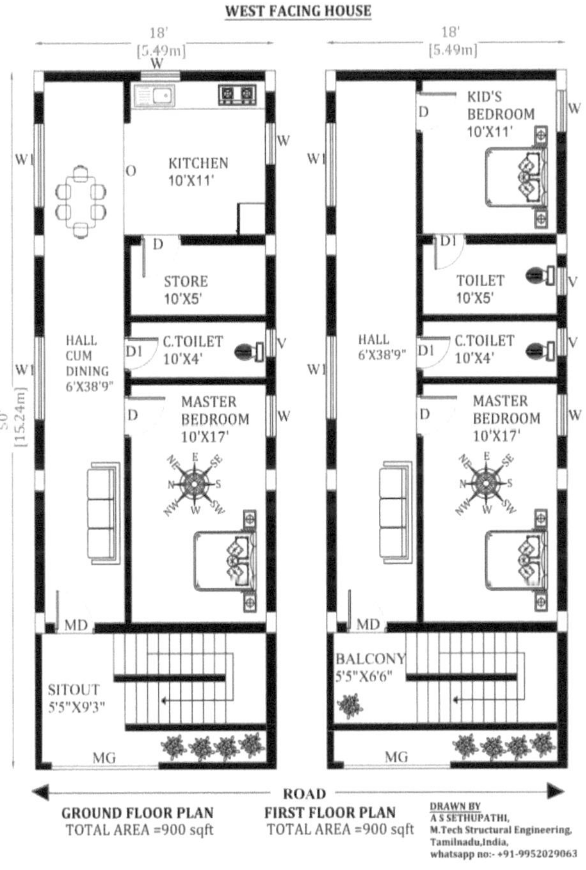

18x50 900 sqft west-facing G+1 House design plan is given in the above image. On the ground floor, the kitchen is placed in the southeast direction. The storeroom is placed near the kitchen is in the south. Hall cum Dining room is placed in the north direction. Common toilet is kept in the south direction. The Master bedroom is placed in the southwest. A portico or sitout is placed in the northwest direction outside of the house.

On the First floor plan, The Hall is available in the north. The Master bedroom is placed in the southwest direction. The kid's bedroom is placed in the southeast direction with an attached toilet is in the south. Common toilet is placed in the south direction. The staircase is placed outside of the house in the southwest direction. The columns are mentioned in this house design are in the size 1'6"x9".Room dimensions are given in this house floor plan very clearly.

30X30 900 SQFT WEST FACING HOUSE PLAN

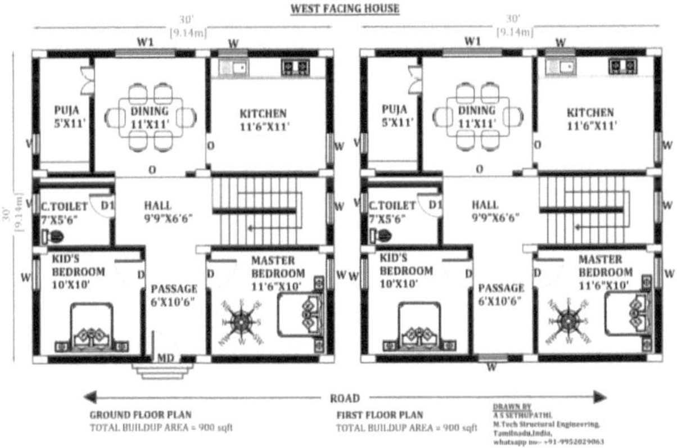

30x30 900 sqft west-facing G+1 Home design plan is given in the above image. On the ground floor, the kitchen is placed in the southeast direction. The dining room is placed in the east near the kitchen. Hall is placed in the center of the house. Pooja's room is kept in the northeast direction. The Master bedroom is kept in the southwest direction. The kid's bedroom is placed in the northwest. A common toilet is available in the north. passage or the Entrance is available in between two bedrooms.

The first floor plans also the same as the ground floor. In

this, The staircase is placed inside of the house in the south direction. The kitchen is placed in the southeast direction. The dining room is placed in the east near the kitchen. Hall is placed in the center of the house. Pooja's room is kept in the northeast direction. The Master bedroom is kept in the southwest direction. The kid's bedroom is placed in the northwest. Common toilet is available in the north. Passage or the Entrance is available in between two bedrooms. The columns are marked in this house design are in the size 1'6"x9". Room dimensions are given in this house floor plan very perfectly.

26X36 936 SQFT WEST FACING HOUSE PLAN

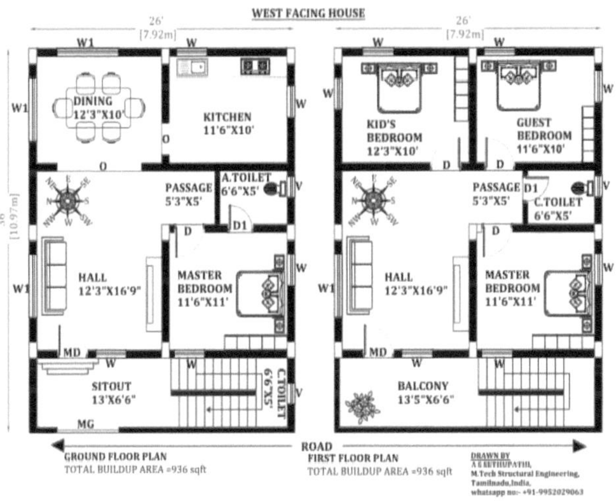

26x36 936 sqft west-facing House design G+1 plan is given in the above image. On the ground floor, the kitchen is placed in the southeast direction. The dining room is placed near the kitchen is in the northeast direction. The living room or the hall is placed in the northwest direction. The Master bedroom is placed in the southwest direction with an attached toilet is in the south direction. The passage is available near the kitchen. Sitout is placed outside of the house is in the northwest. Common toilet is available under the stairs is in the southwest.

On the First floor plan, The hall or living room is available in the northwest. The Master bedroom is placed in the southwest direction. The kid's bedroom is placed in the northeast direction. The guest bedroom is kept in the southeast. The Common toilet is in the south. The staircase is placed outside of the house in the southwest direction. Pillars are mentioned in this house design perfectly is in the size 1'6"x9". Room dimensions are given in this home floor plan very neatly.

36X26 936 SQFT WEST FACING HOUSE PLAN

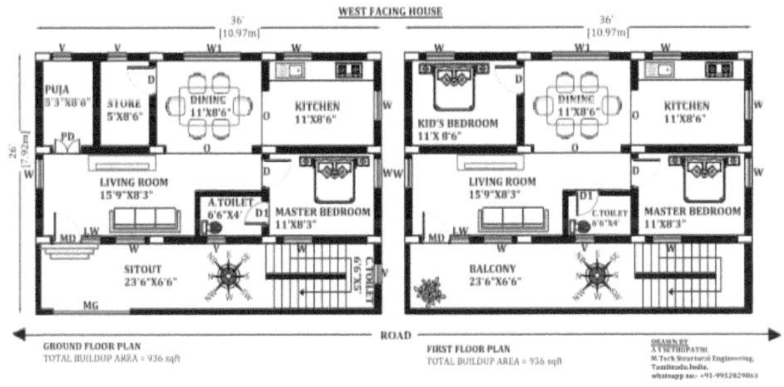

36x26 936 sqft west facing Home design G+1 plan is given in the above image. On the ground floor, the kitchen is placed in the southeast direction. The dining room is placed near the kitchen is in the east direction. The storeroom near the dining is in the east. Puja room is placed in the northeast direction. The living room or the hall is placed in the northwest direction. The Master bedroom is kept in the southwest direction with an attached toilet is in the west direction. Sitout is placed outside of the house is in the northwest. Common toilet is available under the stairs is in the southwest.

On the First floor plan, The hall or living room is available in the northwest. The Master bedroom is placed in the southwest direction. The kid's bedroom is placed in the northeast direction. The Common toilet is in the west. The kitchen is placed in the southeast direction. The dining room is placed near the kitchen is in the east direction. The staircase is placed outside of the house in the southwest direction. The balcony is available in the northwest direction outside of the house. The place of Pillars are specified in this house design perfectly is in the size 1'6"x9". Room dimensions are given in this home floor plan very neatly.

24X40 960 SQFT WEST FACING HOUSE PLAN

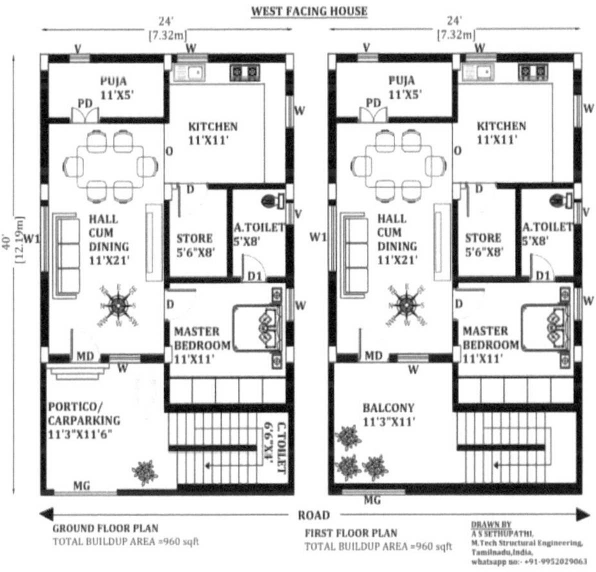

24x40 960 sqft west facing Home design G+1 plan is given in the above image. On the ground floor, the kitchen is placed in the southeast direction. The Hall cum Dining room is placed in the north direction. The storeroom is kept near the kitchen. Pooja's room is kept in the northeast direction. The Master bedroom is kept in the southwest direction with an attached toilet is in the south. Common toilet is available under the stairs is in the southwest. The portico or the car parking space is given in the northwest direction of the home.

The first floor plans also the same as the ground floor. In this, the kitchen is placed in the southeast direction. The Hall cum Dining room is placed in the north direction. The storeroom is kept near the kitchen. Pooja's room is kept in the northeast direction. The Master bedroom is kept in the southwest direction with an attached toilet is in the south. Balcony is available in the northwest direction of the house. The staircase is placed in the southwest. The columns are mentioned in this house design are in the size 1’6”x9”. Room dimensions are given in this home floor plan very neatly.

26X40 1040 SQFT WEST FACING HOUSE PLAN

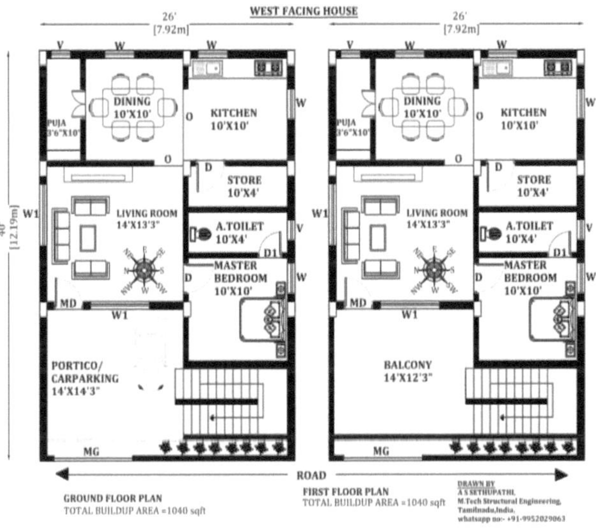

26x40 1040 sqft west-facing G+1 Home plan is given in the above image. On the ground floor, the kitchen is placed in the southeast direction. Dining near the kitchen is placed in the east. The Hall or the living room is placed in the north direction. The storeroom is kept near the kitchen is in the south. Pooja's room is kept in the northeast direction. The Master bedroom is available in the southwest direction with an attached toilet is in the south.

The portico or the car parking space is given in the northwest direction of the house.

The first floor plans also the same as the ground floor. In this, the kitchen is placed in the southeast direction. Dining near the kitchen is placed in the east. The Hall or the living room is placed in the north direction. The storeroom is kept near the kitchen is in the south. Pooja's room is kept in the northeast direction. The Master bedroom is available in the southwest direction with an attached toilet is in the south. A balcony is available in the northwest direction of the house. The staircase is placed in the southwest outside of the house. The columns are specified in this house design are in the size 1'6"x9". Room dimensions are given in this home floor plan very neatly.

33X33 1089 SQFT WEST FACING HOUSE PLAN

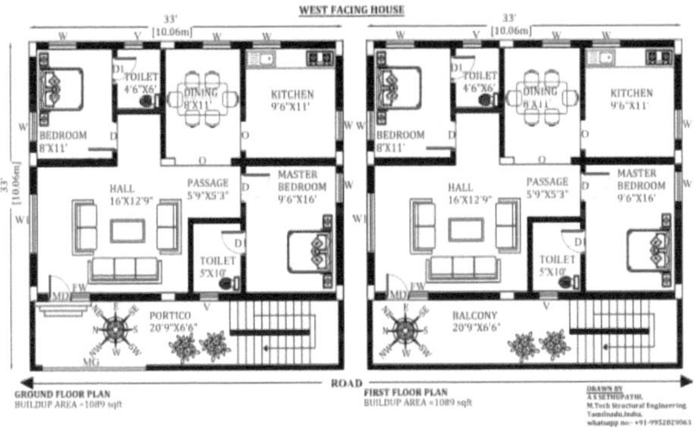

33x33 1089 sqft west-facing G+1 Home plan is given in the above image. On the ground floor, the kitchen is placed in the southeast direction. Dining near the kitchen is placed in the east. The Hall or the living room is placed in the northwest direction. The Master bedroom is available in the southwest direction with an attached toilet is in the west. Children's or the kid's bedroom is available in the northeast direction with an attached toilet is in the east. The passage is available near the bedroom. The portico is in the northwest direction of the house.

The first floor plans also the same as the ground floor. In this, the kitchen is placed in the southeast direction.

Dining near the kitchen is placed in the east. The Hall or the living room is placed in the northwest direction. The Master bedroom is available in the southwest direction with an attached toilet is in the west. Children's or the kid's bedroom is available in the northeast direction with an attached toilet is in the east. The passage is available near the bedroom. Balcony is placed in the northwest direction of the house. The staircase is placed in the southwest outside of the house. The columns are specified in this house design are in the size 1'6"x9". Room dimensions are given in this home floor plan very clearly.

23X50 1150 SQFT WEST FACING HOUSE PLAN

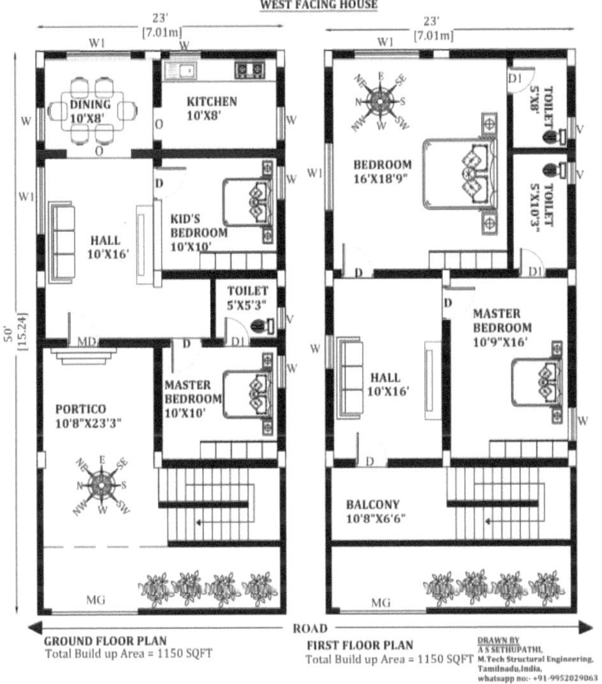

23x50 1150 sqft west-facing G+1 House design plan is given in the above image. On the ground floor, the kitchen is placed in the southeast direction. The dining room is kept in the northeast direction near the kitchen. The living room or the hall is placed in the north. The Master bedroom is placed in the southwest direction with an attached toilet is in the south. the kid's bedroom is placed in the south. A portico or sitout is placed in the northwest direction outside of the house. For gardening, space is available on the west side.

On the First floor plan, The hall or living room is available in the northwest. The Master bedroom is placed in the southwest direction with an attached toilet is in the south. The kid's bedroom is placed in the northeast direction with an attached toilet is in the southeast. A balcony is in the northwest direction. The staircase is placed outside of the house in the southwest direction. The columns are marked in this house design are in the size 1'6"x9".Perfect Room dimensions are given in this home floor plan.

20X60 1200 SQFT WEST FACING HOUSE PLAN

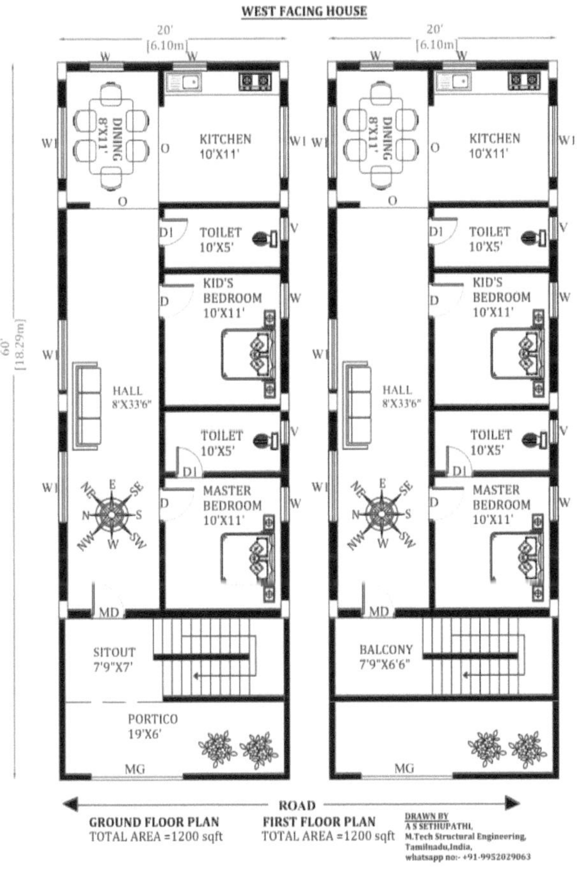

20x60 1200 sqft west-facing G+1 House plan is given in this image. On the ground floor, the kitchen is placed in the southeast direction. Dining near the kitchen is placed in the northeast. The Hall or the living room is placed in the northwest direction. The Master bedroom is available in the southwest direction with an attached toilet is in the south. Children's or the kid's bedroom is available in the south direction. The common toilet is placed in the south. Sitout is placed in the northwest. The portico is available in the west direction of the house.

The first floor plans also the same as the ground floor. In this, the kitchen is placed in the southeast direction. Dining near the kitchen is placed in the northeast. The Hall or the living room is placed in the northwest direction. The Master bedroom is available in the southwest direction with an attached toilet is in the south. Children's or the kid's bedroom is available in the south direction. The common toilet is placed in the south. A balcony is placed in the northwest direction of the house. The staircase is placed in the southwest outside of the house. The pillars are specified in this house design are in the size 1'6"x9". Room dimensions are given in this house floor plan very clearly.

30X40 1200 SQFT WEST FACING HOUSE PLAN

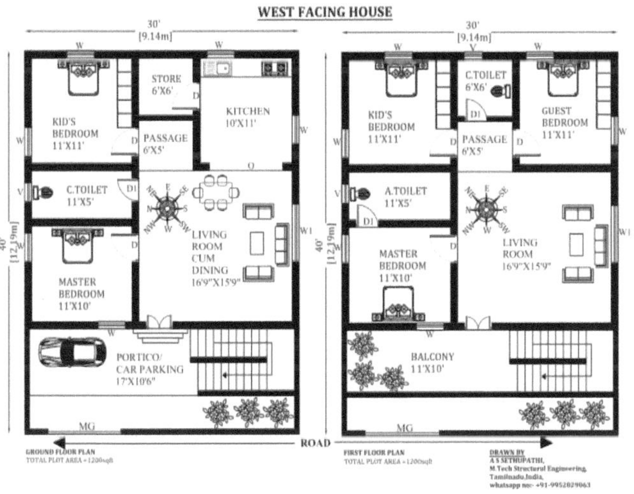

30x40 1200 sqft west-facing House design G+1 plan is given in the above image. On the ground floor, the kitchen is placed in the southeast direction. The storeroom is placed in the east near the kitchen. Living cum Dining room is placed near the kitchen is in the southwest direction. The passage is available near the kitchen. The Master bedroom is placed in the northwest direction. The kid's bedroom is available in the northeast direction.

Common toilet is placed in the north. A portico or car parking is available outside of the house is in the northwest.

On the First floor plan, The hall or living room is available in the southwest. The Master bedroom is placed in the northwest direction with an attached toilet is in the north. The kid's bedroom is kept in the northeast direction. Guest bedroom is kept in the southeast. The Common toilet is placed in the east. The staircase is placed outside of the house in the southwest direction. A balcony is kept in the northwest. Room dimensions are given in this house floor plan very clearly.

40X30 1200 SQFT WEST FACING HOUSE PLAN

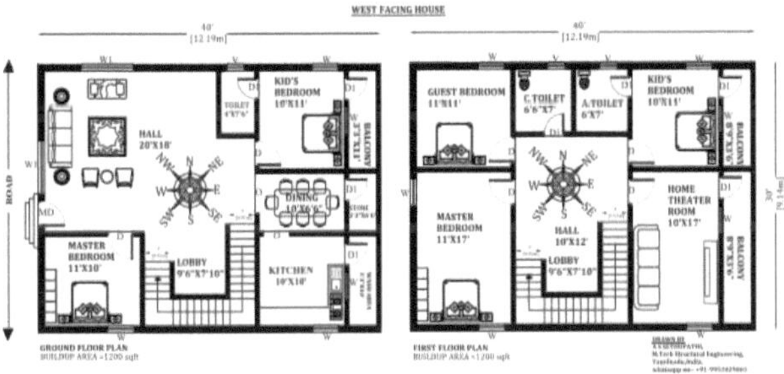

40x30 1200 sqft west facing Home design G+1 plan is given in the above image. On the ground floor, the kitchen is placed in the southeast direction with a wash area nearby. The dining room is available near the kitchen is in the east with the storeroom. The hall or the Living room is placed in the northwest direction. A lobby is available near the staircase inside. The Master bedroom is placed in the southwest direction. The kid's bedroom is available in the northeast direction with a balcony and an attached toilet is kept in the north.

On the First floor plan, The hall or living room is available in the center. The Master bedroom is placed in the southwest direction. The kid's bedroom is available in the northeast direction with a balcony and an attached toilet is kept in the north. Guest bedroom is kept in the northwest. The Common toilet is placed in the north. Home theatre is available in the southeast with an attached balcony. The staircase is placed inside of the house in the south direction. Room dimensions are given in this house floor plan very clearly.

25X50 1250 SQFT WEST FACING HOUSE PLAN

25x50 1250 sqft west-facing G+1 House plan is given in this image. On the ground floor, the kitchen is placed in the southeast direction. Dining near the kitchen is placed in the south. The Hall or the living room is placed in the northwest direction. The Master bedroom is available in the southwest direction with an attached toilet is in the south. Children's or the kid's bedroom is available in the northeast direction. The puja room is placed in the south. The portico is available in the northwest direction of the house. Common toilet is placed under the stairs in the southwest.

The first floor plans also the same as the ground floor. In this, the kitchen is placed in the southeast direction. Dining near the kitchen is placed in the south. The Hall or the living room is placed in the northwest direction. The Master bedroom is available in the southwest direction with an attached toilet is in the south. Children's or the kid's bedroom is available in the northeast direction. The puja room is placed in the south. A balcony is placed in the northwest direction of the house. The staircase is placed in the southwest outside of the house. The pillars are specified in this house plan design are in the size 1'6"x9". Room dimensions are given in this house floor plan very perfectly.

27X50 1350 SQFT WEST FACING HOUSE PLAN

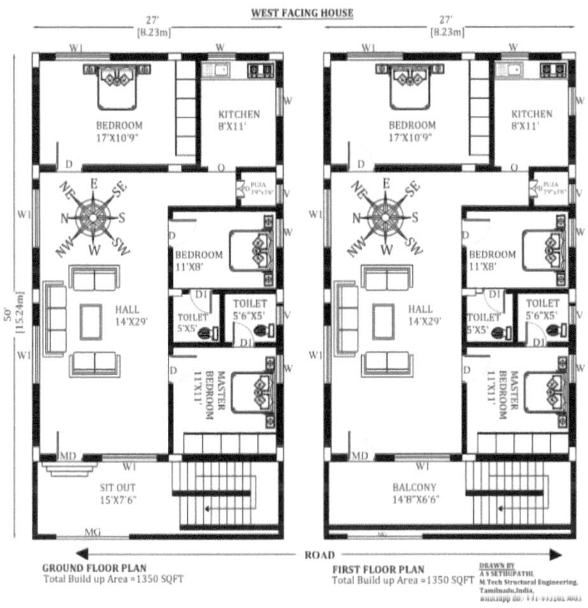

27x50 1350 sqft west-facing G+1 Home plan is given in this image. On the ground floor, the kitchen is placed in the southeast direction. Puja room is available near the kitchen is in the south. The Hall or the living room is placed in the northwest direction. The Master bedroom is available in the southwest direction with an attached toilet is in the south. Children's or the kid's bedroom is available in the south direction with an attached toilet is in the south. A guest bedroom is kept in the northeast direction. The portico or sitout is available in the northwest direction of the house.

The first floor plans also the same as the ground floor. In this plan, the kitchen is placed in the southeast direction. Puja room is available near the kitchen is in the south. The Hall or the living room is placed in the northwest direction. The Master bedroom is available in the southwest direction with an attached toilet is in the south. Children's or the kid's bedroom is available in the south direction with an attached toilet is in the south. A guest bedroom is kept in the northeast direction. Balcony is placed in the northwest direction of the home. The staircase is placed in the southwest outside of the house. The pillars are mentioned in this house plan design are in the size 1'6"x9". Room dimensions are given in this house floor plan very neatly.

35X40 1400 SQFT WEST FACING HOUSE PLAN

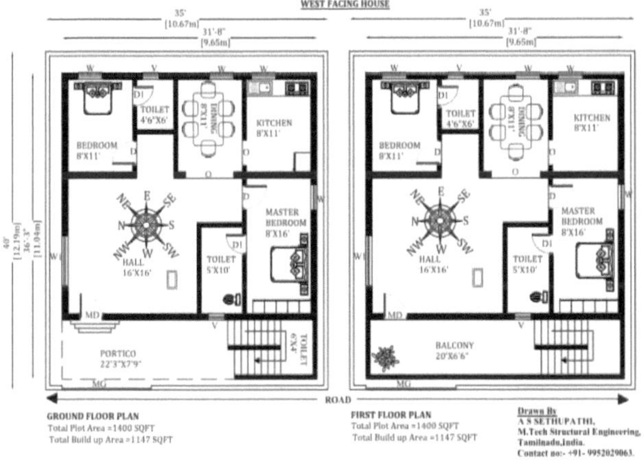

35x40 1400 sqft west-facing G+1 Home design plan is given in this image. On the ground floor plan, the kitchen is placed in the southeast direction. Dining near the kitchen is placed in the east. The Hall or the living room is placed in the northwest direction. The Master bedroom is kept in the southwest direction with an attached toilet is in the west. Children's or the kid's bedroom is available in the northeast direction with an attached toilet is in the east. The portico is available in the northwest direction of the house. Common toilet is placed under the stairs in the southwest.

The first floor plans also the same as the ground floor. In this, the kitchen is placed in the southeast direction. Dining near the kitchen is placed in the east. The Hall or the living room is placed in the northwest direction. The Master bedroom is kept in the southwest direction with an attached toilet is in the west. Children's or the kid's bedroom is available in the northeast direction with an attached toilet is in the east. The Balcony is placed in the northwest direction of the house. The staircase is placed in the southwest outside of the house. Room dimensions are given in this house floor plan very neatly.

30X50 1500 SQFT WEST FACING HOUSE PLAN

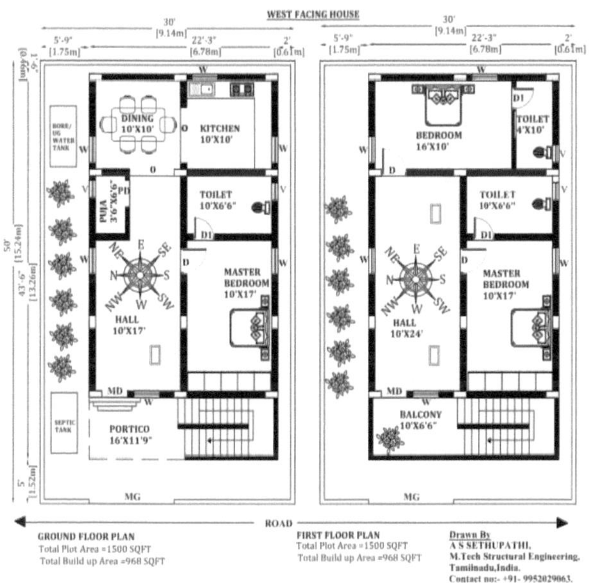

30x50 1500 sqft west-facing G+1 House floor plan is given in the above image. The total buildup area of this plan is 968 sqft. On the ground floor, the kitchen is placed in the southeast direction. The dining room is placed in the northeast near the kitchen. Puja room is kept near the dining is in the north. Hall is placed in the northwest direction. The Master bedroom is kept in the southwest direction with an attached toilet is in the south. Portico is available outside of the house is in the northwest. Septic tank is placed in the north of the northwest direction. Bore or the underground water tank is placed in the northeast direction.

On the First floor plan, The hall or living room is available in the northwest. The Master bedroom is kept in the southwest direction with an attached toilet is in the south. The kid's bedroom is placed in the northeast direction with an attached toilet is in the southeast. The staircase is placed outside of the house in the southwest direction. A balcony is kept in the northwest direction. In this plan, the pillars are marked perfectly. Dimensions are given in this house floor plan very clearly.

30X60 1800 SQFT WEST FACING HOUSE PLAN

30x60 1800 sqft west-facing G+1 Home design plan is given in the above image. On the ground floor, the kitchen is placed in the southeast direction. The dining room is placed in the northeast near the kitchen. The storeroom is available near the kitchen is in the south. Hall is placed in the north direction. Pooja's room is kept in the west direction. The Master bedroom is kept in the southwest direction with an attached toilet is in the south. Sitout is available in the north. Car parking or the portico is placed in the northwest.

In the first floor plan, The staircase is placed inside of the house in the south direction. The kitchen is placed in the southeast direction. The dining room is placed in the northeast near the kitchen. A common toilet is available near the kitchen is in the south. Hall is placed in the north direction. The Master bedroom is kept in the southwest direction with an attached toilet is in the south. Kid's bedroom is placed in the north with an attached toilet is in the northwest. The columns are placed in this house design are in the size 1'6"x9". Room dimensions are given in this home floor plan very perfectly. The staircase is available inside of the house is in the south direction.

36X50 1800 SQFT WEST FACING HOUSE PLAN

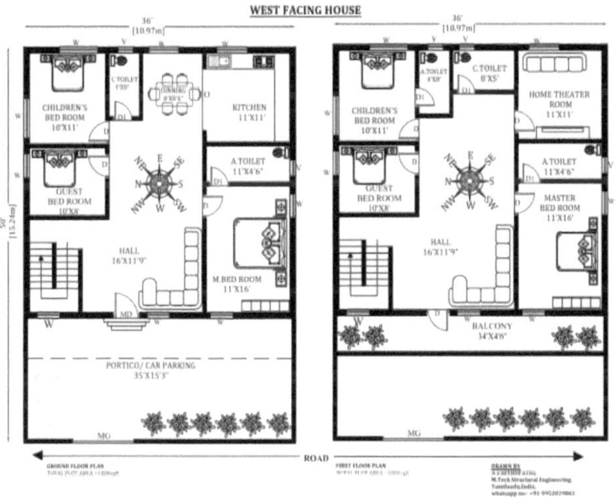

36x50 1800 sqft west facing Home G+1 plan is given in the above image. On the ground floor, the kitchen is placed in the southeast direction. The dining room is available near the kitchen is in the east. The hall or the Living room is placed in the west direction. The Master bedroom is placed in the southwest direction with an attached toilet is in the south. Kid's or the children's bedroom is available in the northeast direction. Guest bedroom is placed in the north. Common toilet is available in the east. A portico or car parking is available in the southwest.

On the First floor plan, The hall or the Living room is placed in the west direction. The Master bedroom is placed in the southwest direction with an attached toilet is in the south. Kid's or the children's bedroom is available in the northeast direction with an attached toilet is in the east. Guest bedroom is placed in the north direction. Common toilet is available in the east. Home theatre is available in the southeast. The staircase is placed inside of the house is in the northwest direction. A balcony is placed in the west direction. Room dimensions are given in this house floor plan very clearly.

45X45 2025 SQFT WEST FACING HOUSE PLAN

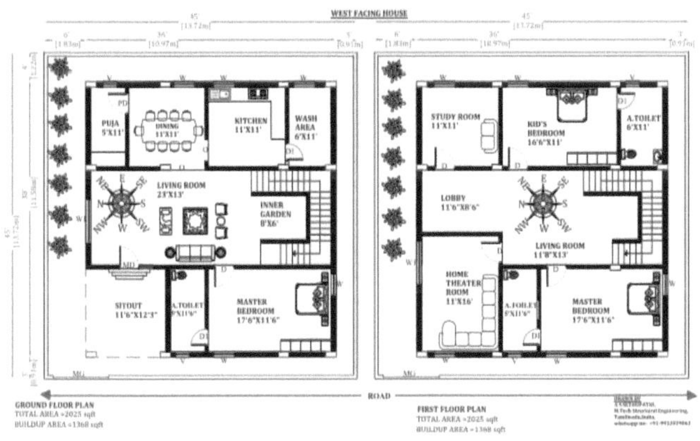

45x 45 2025 sqft G+1 west facing Home plan is given in the above image. On the ground floor, the kitchen is placed in the east direction with a wash area nearby is in the southeast. The dining room is available near the kitchen is in the east. Puja room is kept in the northeast direction. The hall or the Living room is placed in the north direction. Inner Garden is available near the staircase. The Master bedroom is placed in the southwest direction with an attached toilet is kept in the west. Sitout is available in the northwest direction.

On the First floor plan, The hall or living room is available in the center. The lobby is in the north. The Master bedroom is placed in the southwest direction with an attached toilet is kept in the west. The kid's bedroom is available in the east direction with an attached toilet is kept in the southeast. The study room is kept in the northeast. Home theatre is available in the northwest. The staircase is placed inside of the house in the south direction. Room dimensions are given in this house floor plan perfectly.

40X60 2400 SQFT WEST FACING HOUSE PLAN

40x 60 2400 sqft G+1 west-facing House plan is given in the above image. On the ground floor plan, the kitchen is placed in the south direction with an attached utility room is in the southeast. A lobby is available near the kitchen. Hall cum Dining room is available in the north. Entrance is available in the northwest. The Master bedroom is placed in the southwest direction with an attached toilet is kept in the west. A guest bedroom is available in the east with an attached toilet is in the east. The drawing room is kept in the northeast. Sitout is available in the northwest direction. A portico or the car parking is in the west direction.

On the First floor plan, The hall or living room is available in the north. The lobby is placed in the south. The Master bedroom is placed in the southwest direction with an attached toilet is kept in the west. The kid's bedroom is available in the east direction with an attached toilet is kept in the east. Guest bedroom is placed in the south with an attached balcony is in the southeast. A study room is kept in the northeast. The foyer is available in the northwest. A balcony is available on the west side. The staircase is placed inside of the house in the south direction. Room dimensions are given in this house floor plan perfectly. Furnitures are placed in this floor plan neatly.

60X40 2400 SQFT WEST FACING HOUSE PLAN

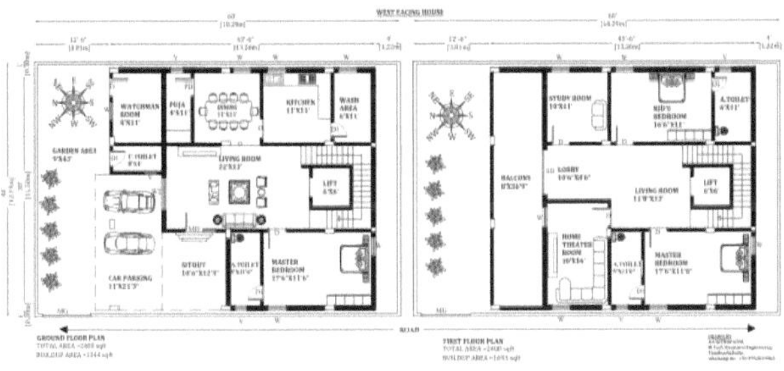

60x 40 2400 sqft west-facing G+1 House plan is given in the above image. On the ground floor plan, the kitchen is placed in the south direction with an attached wash area is in the southeast. The dining room is placed on the east side near the kitchen. Puja room is kept near the dining is in the east. The living room or the Hall is available in the north. The Master bedroom is placed in the southwest direction with an attached toilet is kept in the west. Watchman room is available outside is in the northeast. Common toilet is placed near the watchman room is in the north. Sitout is available in the west direction. A portico or the car parking is in the northwest direction. The Garden area is available in the north direction.

On the First floor plan, The hall or living room is available in the center. The lobby is placed in the north. The Master bedroom is placed in the southwest direction with an attached toilet is kept in the west. The kid's bedroom is available in the east direction with an attached toilet is kept in the southeast. The Home theatre room is placed in the northwest. A study room is kept in the northeast. A balcony is available on the north side. The staircase and the lift are placed inside of the house in the south direction. Room dimensions are given in this home floor plan very perfectly. Items of Furniture are placed in this floor plan neatly. Columns are marked in this floor plan nicely.

NORTH FACING HOUSE PLANS

22X22 484 SQFT NORTH FACING HOUSE PLAN

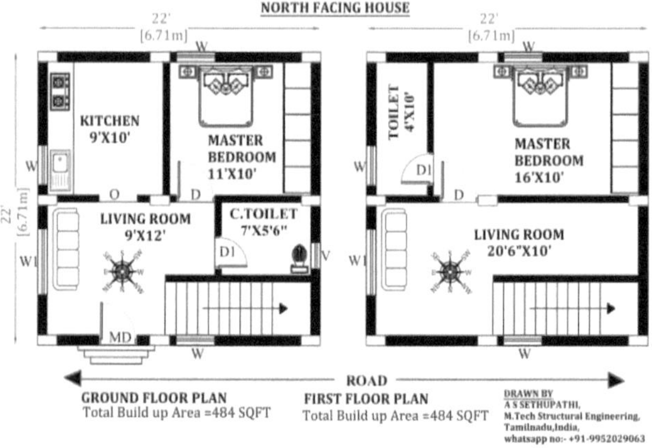

22x22 484 sqft north-facing G+1 small House Plan is shown in the above image. On the ground floor plan, the kitchen is in the southeast direction. The Master Bedroom is placed in the southwest direction. Hall is in the Northeast direction. Common toilet is available in the west direction. In the First floor plan, the Master bedroom is in the southwest direction with an attached toilet is available in the southeast. The living room is placed in the northeast. The staircase is available in the northwest direction inside of the house. Pillars are marked in this small home plan in the size of 1'6"x9".This home design plan is useful for people who searching for small house plan ideas.

20X30 600 SQFT NORTH FACING HOUSE PLAN

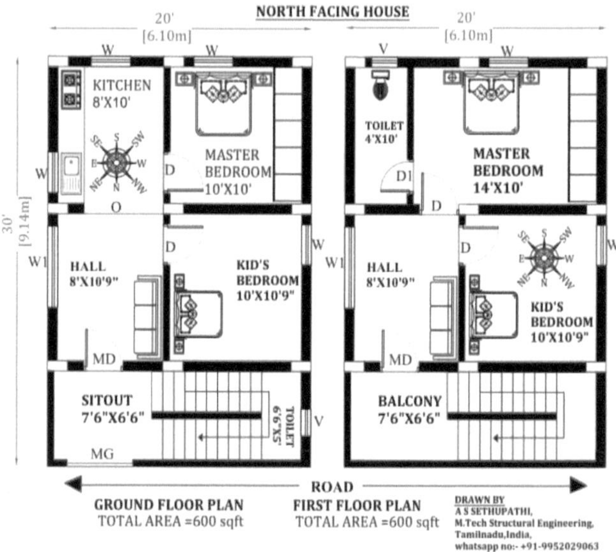

20x30 600 sqft north-facing House plan with Furniture Design is given in the above image. In this G+1 home design ground floor plan, the kitchen is placed in the southeast direction. The Master bedroom is placed in the southwest direction. Kid's Bedroom is in the northwest direction. The Hall or the living room is in the northeast direction. The toilet is available outside of the house under the stairs. The sitout is available outside of the house in the northeast direction.

On the First floor plan, The Master bedroom is placed in the southwest direction with an attached toilet is in the southeast. Kid's Bedroom is placed in the northwest direction. The Hall or the living room is in the northeast direction. Moreover, the balcony is available in the northeast direction. The Staircase is placed outside of the house in the northwest direction. Furniture details are given as per the vastu shastra. pillars are mentioned in this house plan and its size is 1'6"x9".

30X20 600 SQFT NORTH FACING HOUSE PLAN

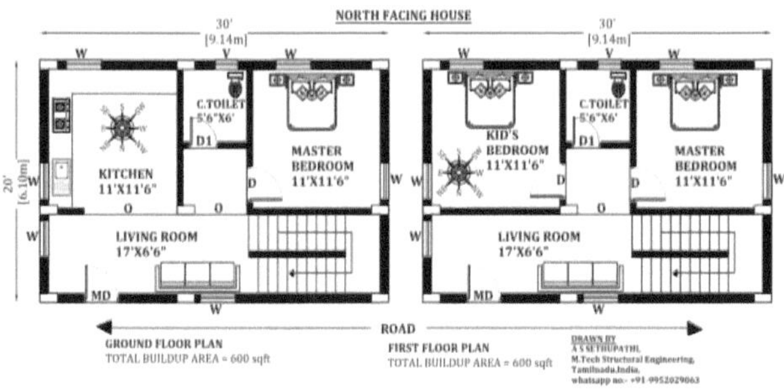

30x20 600 sqft North facing G+1 small duplex House Plan is shown in the above image. In the ground floor plan, the kitchen is in the southeast direction. The Master Bedroom is placed in the southwest direction. The common toilet is placed in the south direction. The living room is in the Northeast direction.

On the First floor plan, The Master Bedroom is placed in the southwest direction. The kid's bedroom is kept in the southeast direction. The common toilet is placed in the south direction. The living room is available in the northeast direction. The Staircase is placed in the northwest direction inside of the house. Pillars are mentioned in this home plan in the size of 1'6"x9".This home design plan is useful for people who searching for tiny duplex house plan ideas.

25X25 625 SQFT NORTH FACING HOUSE PLAN

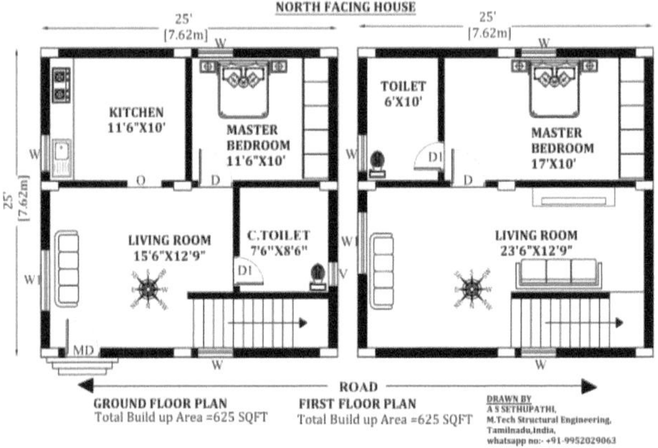

25x25 625 sqft north-facing G+1 tiny House Plan is shown in the above image. On the ground floor plan, the kitchen is in the southeast direction. The Master Bedroom is placed in the southwest direction. Hall is in the Northeast direction. Common toilet is available in the west direction. In the First floor plan, the Master bedroom is in the southwest direction with an attached toilet is available in the southeast. The living room is placed in the north. The staircase is available in the northwest direction inside of the house. Pillars are marked in this tiny home plan in the size of 1’6”x9”.This home design plan is useful for people who searching for tiny house plan ideas.

26X26 676 SQFT NORTH FACING HOUSE PLAN

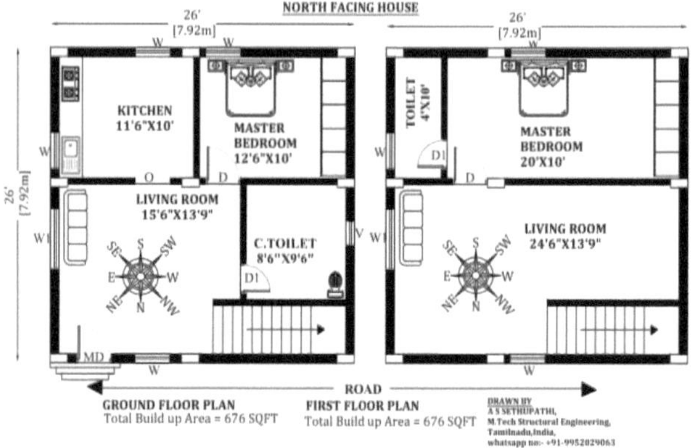

26x26 676 sqft north-facing G+1 tiny Home Plan design is shown in the above image. On the ground floor plan, the kitchen is in the southeast direction. The Master Bedroom is placed in the southwest direction. The living room is in the Northeast direction. Common toilet is available in the west direction. In the First floor plan, the Master bedroom is in the southwest direction with an attached toilet is available in the southeast. The living room is placed in the north. The staircase is available in the northwest direction inside of the house. Pillars are marked in this tiny home plan design in the size of 1'6"x9".This house design plan is useful for people who searching for tiny home plan ideas.

20X40 800 SQFT NORTH FACING HOUSE PLAN

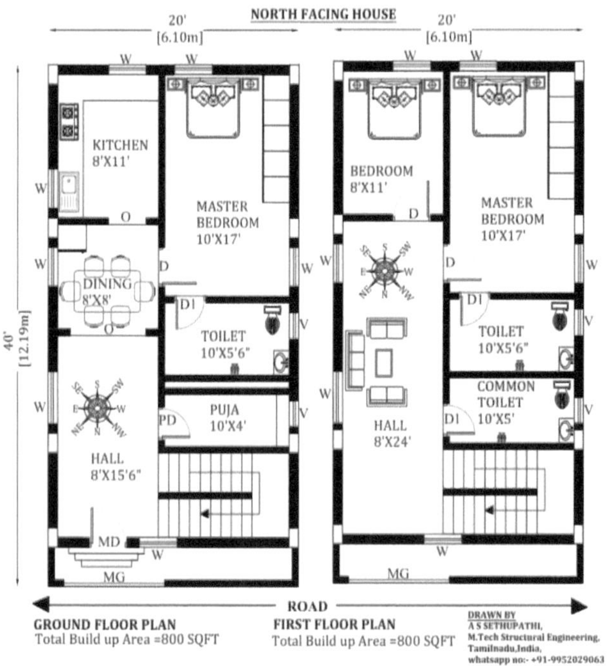

20x40 800 sqft G+1 north-facing duplex Home design plan is given in this image. On the ground floor, the kitchen is set in the southeast direction. Dining near the kitchen is in the east direction. The Master bedroom is placed in the southwest direction with an attached toilet is in the west. On the toilet, the person wanna sit facing north or south direction as per vastu shastra. Puja room is available in the west. The hall is available in the northeast direction.

On the First floor, The hall or living room is available in the northeast direction. The Master bedroom is situated in the southwest direction with an attached toilet is in the west. The kid's bedroom is placed in the southeast direction. The common bathroom is placed in the west. The staircase is placed inside the house in the northwest direction. Pillars are marked in this home design plan are in the size 1'6"x9".

22X40 880 SQFT NORTH FACING HOUSE PLAN

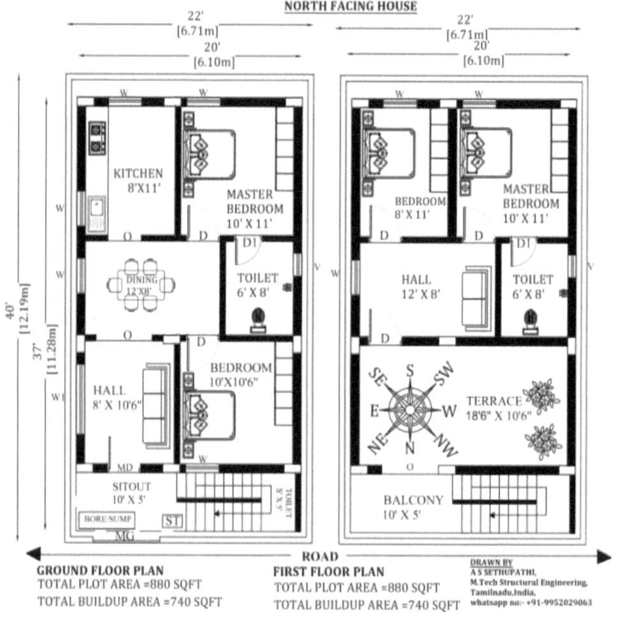

22x40 880 sqft G+1 north-facing House design plan is given in the above image. On the ground floor, the kitchen is set in the southeast direction. Dining near the kitchen is in the east direction. The Master bedroom is placed in the southwest direction with an attached toilet is in the west. The children's bedroom is available in the northwest direction. The hall is available in the northeast direction. Sitout is placed in the northeast outside of the home. The details of the Septic tank are given in this plan, and it is placed in the north direction. Borewell or sump is placed in the northeast direction.

On the First floor, The hall or living room is available in the northeast. The Master bedroom is positioned in the southwest direction with an attached toilet is in the west. The kid's bedroom is placed in the southeast direction. The open terrace is available in the north. The staircase is placed outside of the house in the northwest direction. Pillars are marked in this home design plan are in the size 1'6"x9".

18X50 900 SQFT NORTH FACING HOUSE PLAN

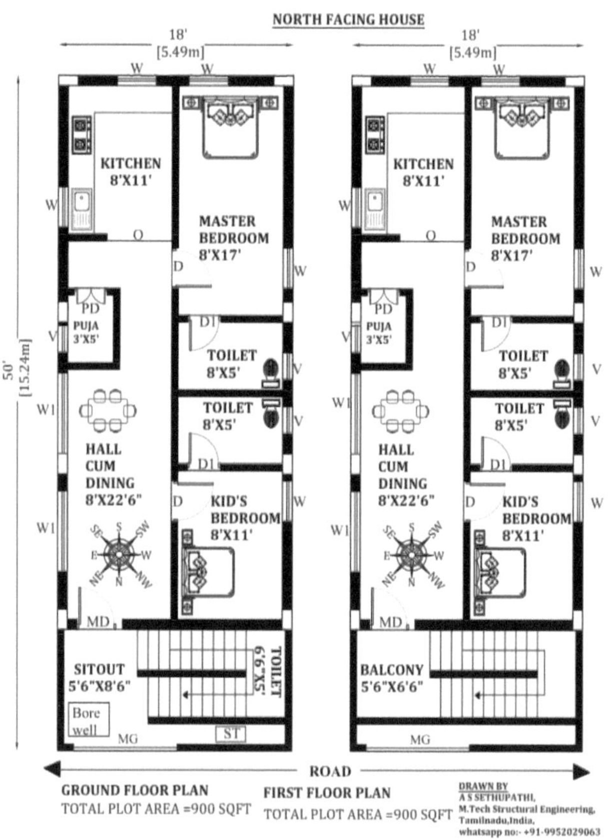

18x50 900 sqft G+1 North House design plan is given in this image. On the ground floor, the kitchen is provided in the southeast direction. The Master bedroom is placed in the southwest direction with an attached toilet is in the west. The children's bedroom is available in the northwest direction with an attached toilet is in the west. Puja's room is kept on the east side. The hall cum dining is available in the northeast direction. Sitout is placed in the northeast outside of the home. Common toilet is kept in the northwest under the stairs outside. The Septic tank is placed in the northwest direction. Borewell is placed in the northeast direction.

The first-floor plan also the same as the ground floor. In this first floor plan, the kitchen is placed in the southeast direction. The Master bedroom is placed in the southwest direction with an attached toilet is in the west. The children's bedroom is available in the northwest direction with an attached toilet is in the west. Puja room is placed on the east side. The hall cum dining is available in the northeast direction. The balcony is placed in the northeast outside of the home. The staircase is placed in the northwest outside of the house. Room dimensions are given perfectly in this plan. Pillars are also marked clearly in this house plan.

30X30 900 SQFT NORTH FACING HOUSE PLAN

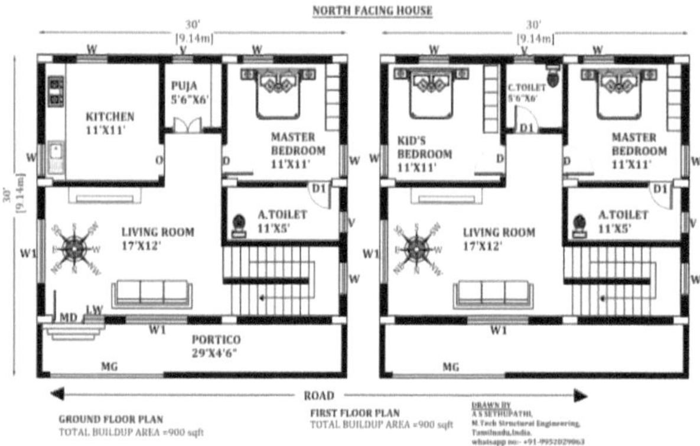

30x30 900 sqft G+1 north-facing duplex House design plan is given in this image. On this ground floor plan, the kitchen is positioned in the southeast direction. The Master bedroom is placed in the southwest direction with an attached toilet is in the west. Puja room is available in the south. The hall or living room is available in the northeast direction.

On the First floor, The hall or living room is available in the northeast direction. The Master bedroom is placed in the southwest direction with an attached toilet is in the west. The kid's bedroom is placed in the southeast direction. The common bathroom is placed in the south. The staircase is placed inside the house in the northwest direction. Pillars are marked in this home design are in the size 1'6"x9".

26X36 936 SQFT NORTH FACING HOUSE PLAN

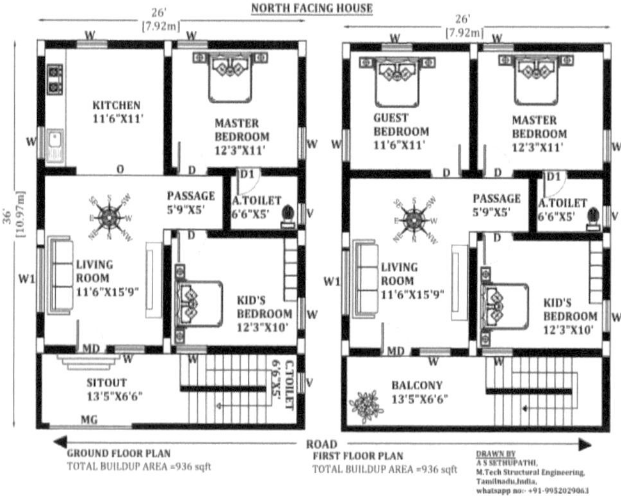

26x36 936 sqft G+1 North facing House design plan is given in the above image. On the ground floor, the kitchen is set in the southeast direction. The Master bedroom is placed in the southwest direction with an attached toilet is in the west. Children's or kid's bedroom is available in the northwest direction. The hall or living room is available in the northeast direction. Sitout is placed in the northeast outside of the house. A common toilet is available under the staircase is in the northwest direction.

On the First floor, The hall or living room is available in the northeast. The Master bedroom is provided in the southwest direction with an attached toilet is in the west. The kid's bedroom is placed in the northwest direction. The guest bedroom is available in the southwest. The staircase is placed outside of the house in the northwest direction. Pillars are marked in this home design are in the size 1'6"x9". Room dimensions are given clearly in this plan.

36X26 936 SQFT NORTH FACING HOUSE PLAN

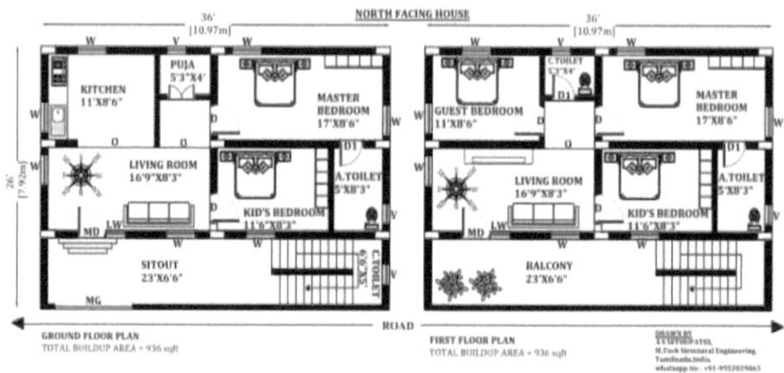

36x26 936 sqft G+1 North facing House design plan is given in the above image. On the ground floor, the kitchen is provided in the southeast direction. The Master bedroom is placed in the southwest direction with an attached toilet is in the northwest. Children's or kid's bedroom is available in the north direction. Puja room is in the south. The living room is available in the northeast direction. Sitout is placed in the northeast outside of the house. A common toilet is available under the staircase is in the northwest direction.

On the First floor, The Master bedroom is placed in the southwest direction with an attached toilet is in the northwest. The kid's bedroom is placed in the north direction. The guest bedroom is available in the southwest. Common toilet is kept in the south. The hall or living room is available in the northeast. The staircase is placed outside of the house in the northwest direction. Pillars are mentioned in this home design are in the size 1'6"x9". Room dimensions are given perfectly in this plan.

24X40 960 SQFT NORTH FACING HOUSE PLAN

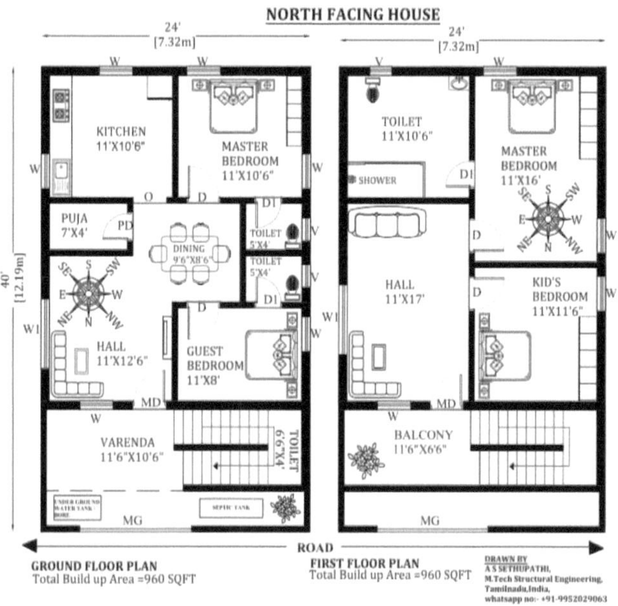

24x40 960 sqft G+1 north Home design plan is given in this image. On the ground floor, the kitchen is set in the southeast direction. Dining is the available center of the house near the kitchen. The Master bedroom is placed in the southwest direction with an attached toilet is in the west. The guest bedroom is available in the northwest direction with an attached toilet is in the west. Puja room is placed on the east side. The hall is available in the northeast direction. varenda is placed in the northeast outside of the house. A common toilet is available under the staircase is in the northwest direction. The Septic tank is placed in the northwest direction. Borewell and the underground water tank are placed in the northeast direction.

On the first floor plan, The Master bedroom is placed in the southwest direction with an attached toilet is in the southeast. Children's or the kid's bedroom is available in the northwest direction with an attached toilet is in the west. The living room or the hall is available in the northeast direction. The balcony is placed in the northeast outside of the home. Staircase is placed in the northwest outside of the house. Room dimensions are given perfectly in this home plan.

26X40 1040 SQFT NORTH FACING HOUSE PLAN

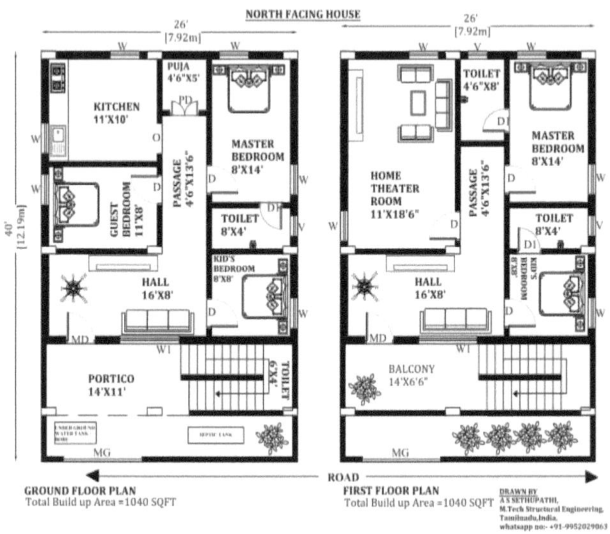

26x40 1040 sqft G+1 North House design plan is given in this image. On the ground floor, the kitchen is situated in the southeast direction. The Master bedroom is placed in the southwest direction with an attached toilet is in the west. The guest bedroom is available in the east. The kid's bedroom is in the northwest direction. Puja room is placed on the south side. The hall is available in the northeast direction. portico is placed in the northeast outside of the house. A common toilet is available under the staircase is in the northwest direction. The Septic tank is placed in the northwest direction. Borewell and the underground water tank are placed in the northeast direction.

On the first floor plan, The Master bedroom is placed in the southwest direction with an attached toilet is in the south. Children's or the kid's bedroom is available in the northwest direction with an attached toilet is in the west. Home theatre is placed in the southeast direction. The living room or the hall is available in the northeast direction. The balcony is placed in the northeast outside of the home. Staircase is placed in the northwest outside of the house. Room dimensions are given clearly in this home plan. Pillars are also marked in this house plan.

33X33 1089 SQFT NORTH FACING HOUSE PLAN

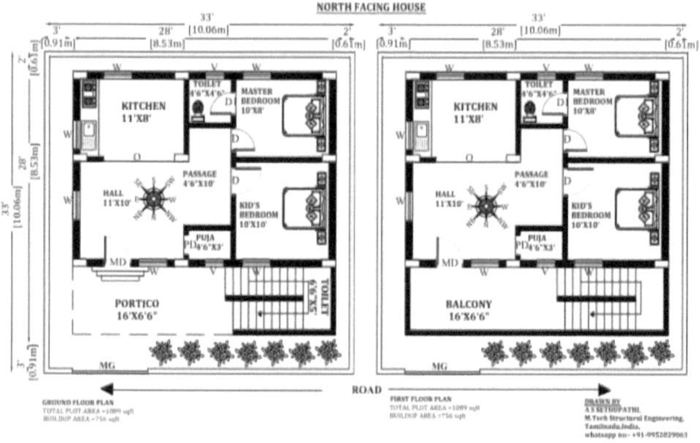

33x33 1089 sqft G+1 North House design plan is given in this image. On the ground floor, the kitchen is set in the southeast direction. The Master bedroom is placed in the southwest direction with an attached toilet is in the south. The kid's bedroom is in the northwest direction. Puja room is placed on the north side. The hall is available in the northeast direction. portico is placed in the northeast outside of the house. A common toilet is available under the staircase is in the northwest direction.

The first-floor plan also the same as the ground floor plan.

On the First floor plan, the kitchen is placed in the southeast direction. The Master bedroom is placed in the southwest direction with an attached toilet is in the south. The kid's bedroom is in the northwest direction. Puja room is placed on the north side. The hall is available in the northeast direction. The balcony is placed in the northeast outside of the house. The column details and room dimensions are given perfectly in this plan. The staircase is placed outside of the home is in the northwest direction.

23X50 1150 SQFT NORTH FACING HOUSE PLAN

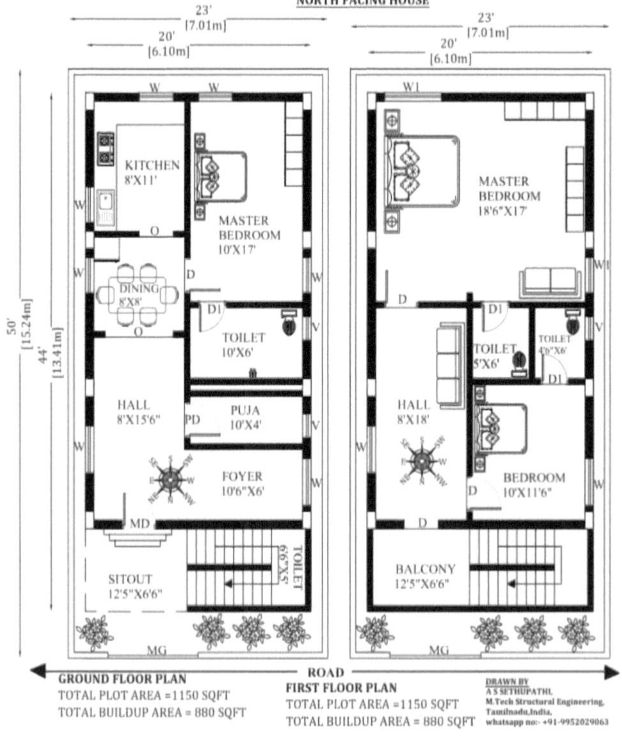

23x50 1150 sqft G+1 north-facing Home design plan is given in this image. On the ground floor plan, the kitchen is provided in the southeast direction. Dining near the kitchen is in the east direction. The Master bedroom is placed in the southwest direction with an attached toilet is in the west. Puja room is available in the west direction. The hall is available in the northeast direction. Sitout is placed in the northeast outside of the home. The foyer is available in the northwest. sitout is placed in the northeast outside of the house. A common toilet is available under the staircase is in the northwest direction.

On the First floor, The hall or living room is available in the northeast. The Master bedroom is placed in the southwest direction with an attached toilet is in the west. The kid's bedroom is placed in the northwest direction with an attached toilet is in the west. The balcony is available in the northeast. The staircase is placed outside of the house in the northwest direction. Pillars are marked in this home design plan are in the size 1'6"x9".

20X60 1200 SQFT NORTH FACING HOUSE PLAN

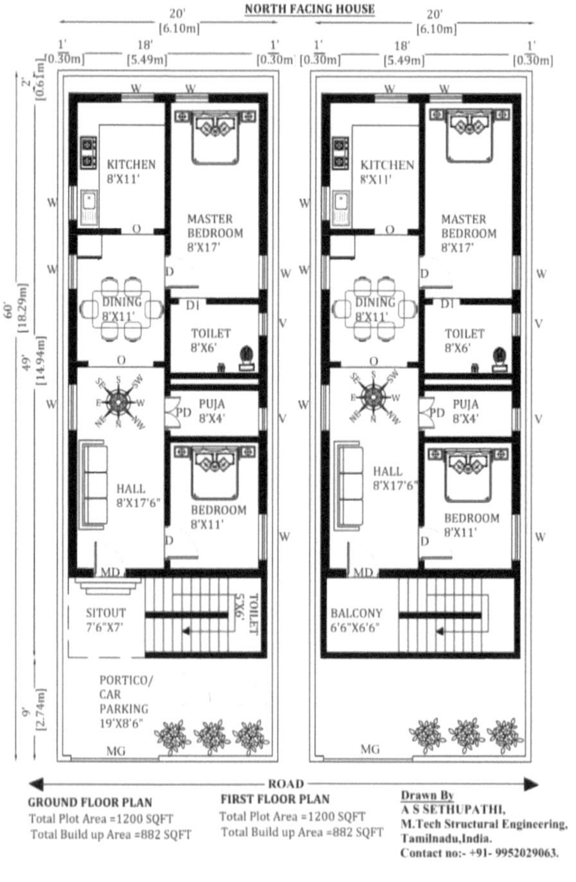

20x60 1200 sqft G+1 north-facing House design plan is given in this image. On the ground floor plan, the kitchen is positioned in the southeast direction. Dining near the kitchen is in the east direction. The Master bedroom is placed in the southwest direction with an attached toilet is in the west. The kid's bedroom or the children's bedroom is placed in the northwest. Puja room is available in the west direction. The hall is available in the northeast direction. Sitout is placed in the northeast outside of the home. Portico or car parking is available in the north. sitout is placed in the northeast outside of the house. A common toilet is available under the staircase is in the northwest direction.

The first floor also the same as the ground floor plan, In this, the kitchen is placed in the southeast direction. Dining near the kitchen is in the east direction. The Master bedroom is placed in the southwest direction with an attached toilet is in the west. The kid's bedroom or the children's bedroom is placed in the northwest. Puja room is available in the west direction. The hall is available in the northeast direction. The balcony is available in the northeast. The staircase is placed outside of the house in the northwest direction. Room dimensions are mentioned clearly.

30X40 1200 SQFT NORTH FACING HOUSE PLAN

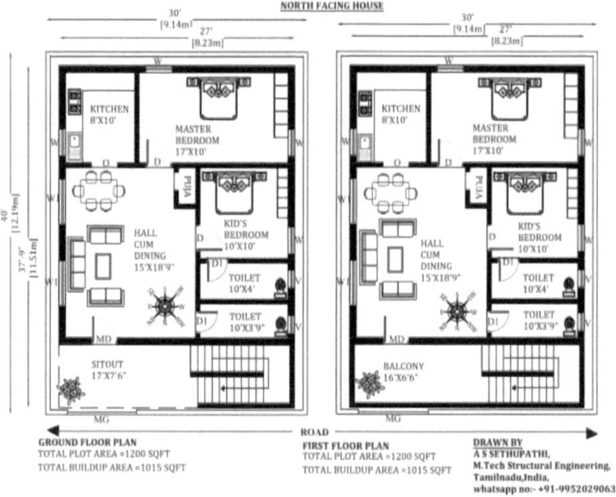

30x40 1200 sqft G+1 north-facing House plan is given in this image. On the ground floor plan, the kitchen is placed in the southeast direction. The hall cum dining is available in the northeast direction The Master bedroom is placed in the southwest direction. The kid's bedroom or the children's bedroom is placed in the west with an attached toilet is in the west. Puja room is available in the west direction. Common toilet is placed in the northwest direction. Sitout is placed in the northeast outside of the house.

The first floor also the same as the ground floor plan, In this, the kitchen is placed in the southeast direction. The hall cum dining is provided in the northeast direction The Master bedroom is placed in the southwest direction. The kid's bedroom or the children's bedroom is placed in the west with an attached toilet is in the west. Puja room is available in the west direction. Common toilet is placed in the northwest direction. The balcony is available in the northeast. The staircase is placed outside of the house in the northwest direction. Room dimensions are mentioned in this plan perfectly.

40X30 1200 SQFT NORTH FACING HOUSE PLAN

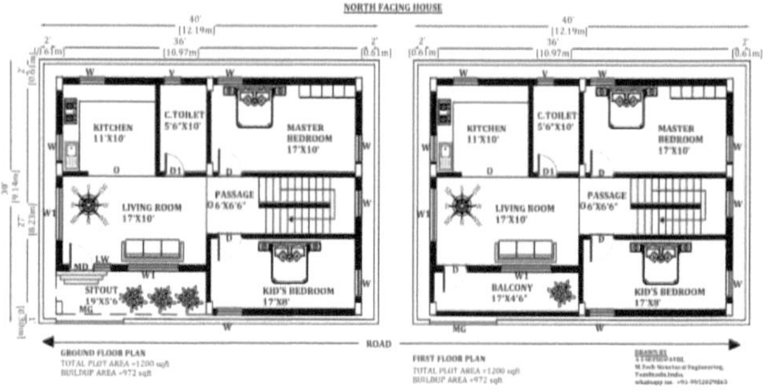

40x30 1200 sqft G+1 North House design plan is given in this image. On the ground floor, the kitchen is situated in the southeast direction. The Master bedroom is placed in the southwest direction. The kid's bedroom is in the northwest direction. The hall or Living room is available in the northeast direction. portico or sitout is placed in the northeast outside of the house. Common toilet is available in the south direction.

The first-floor plan also the same as the ground floor plan. On the First floor plan, the kitchen is placed in the southeast direction. The Master bedroom is placed in the southwest direction. The kid's bedroom is in the northwest direction. The hall or Living room is available in the northeast direction. Common toilet is available in the south direction. The balcony is placed in the northeast outside of the house. The column details and room dimensions are given perfectly in this plan. The staircase is placed inside of the home is in the west direction.

25X50 1250 SQFT NORTH FACING HOUSE PLAN

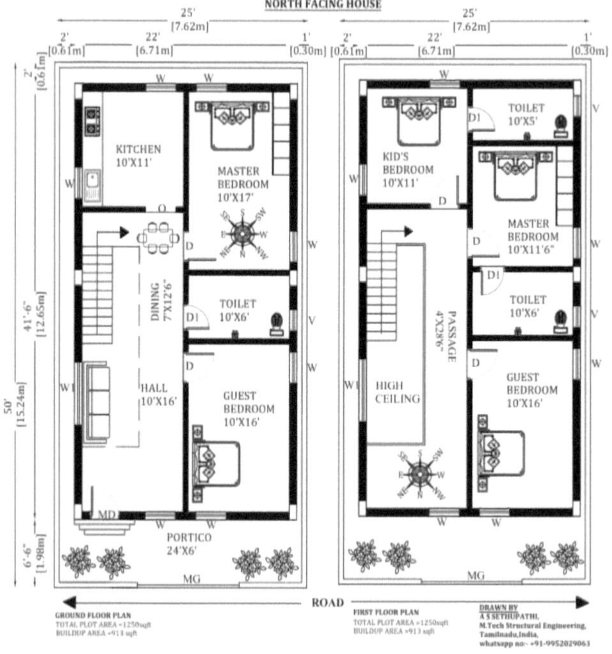

25x50 1250 sqft G+1 north Home design plan is given in this image. On the ground floor, the kitchen is set in the southeast direction. Dining is available in the east near the staircase. The Master bedroom is placed in the southwest direction. The guest bedroom is available in the northwest direction. The hall is available in the northeast direction. Veranda or portico is placed in the north outside of the house. Common toilet is available in the west direction.

On the first floor plan, The Master bedroom is placed in the west direction with an attached toilet is in the west. Children's or the kid's bedroom is available in the southeast direction with an attached toilet is in the southwest. The guest bedroom is available in the northwest direction. A high ceiling is available in the east direction. The staircase is placed in the east inside of the house. Room dimensions are given perfectly in this home plan. Pillars are also marked clearly in this house plan.

27X50 1350 SQFT NORTH FACING HOUSE PLAN

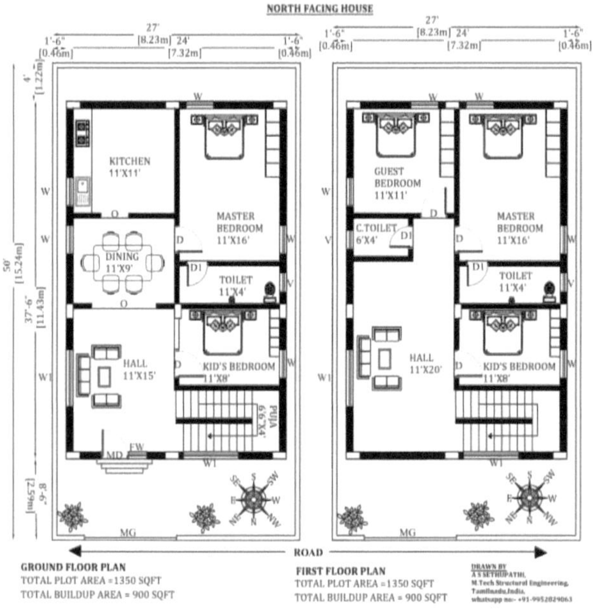

27x50 1350 sqft G+1 north-facing Home design floor plan is given in the above image. On the ground floor plan, the kitchen is placed in the southeast direction. Dining near the kitchen is in the east direction. The Master bedroom is placed in the southwest direction with an attached toilet is in the west. Children's or kid's bedroom is available in the west direction. The hall is available in the northeast direction. Puja room is kept in the northwest under the staircase. Sitout is placed in the north outside of the home. In this plan, you can place the septic tank in the northwest direction. Borewell or sump you can place in the northeast direction.

On the First floor, The hall or living room is available in the northeast. The Master bedroom is positioned in the southwest direction with an attached toilet is in the west. The kid's bedroom is placed in the west direction. The guest bedroom is kept in the southeast direction. Common toilet is placed in the east. The staircase is placed inside of the house in the northwest direction. Pillars are marked in this home design plan perfectly is in the size 1'6"x9".

35X40 1400 SQFT NORTH FACING HOUSE PLAN

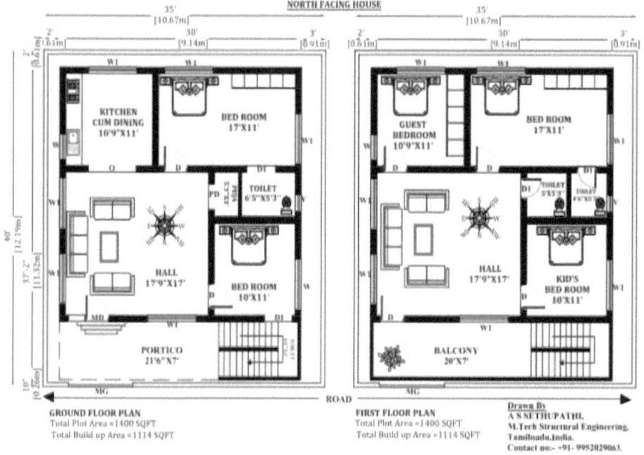

35x40 1400 sqft north-facing G+1 Home design floor plan is given in the above image. On the ground floor plan, the kitchen cum dining is kept in the southeast direction. The Master bedroom is placed in the southwest direction with an attached toilet is in the west. Children's or kid's bedroom is available in the northwest direction. The hall is available in the northeast direction. Puja's room is kept on the west side. portico is placed in the northeast outside of the home. Common toilet is available under the staircase is in the northwest direction. In this plan, you can place the septic tank in the north or northwest direction near the staircase. Borewell or underground water tank you can place in the northeast direction.

On the First floor, The hall or living room is available in the northeast. The Master bedroom is placed in the southwest direction with an attached toilet is in the west. The kid's bedroom is placed in the northwest direction. The guest bedroom is kept in the southeast direction. Common toilet is placed in the west. The staircase is placed outside of the house in the northwest direction.

30X50 1500 SQFT NORTH FACING HOUSE PLAN

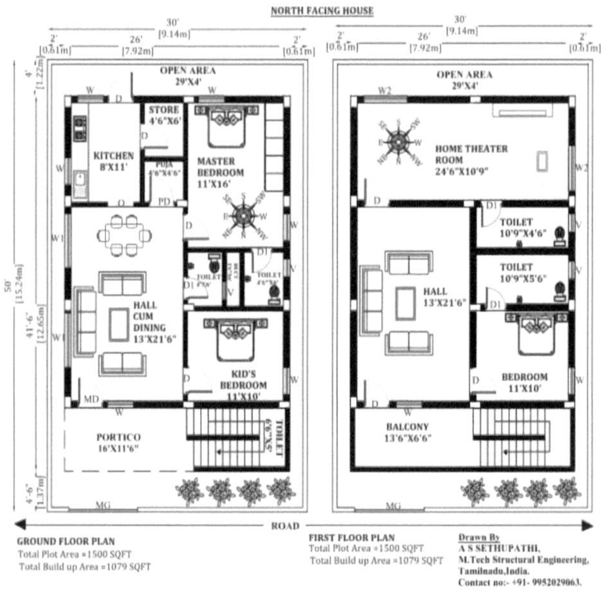

30x50 1500 sqft north-facing G+1 House design floor plan is given in the above image. On the ground floor plan, the kitchen is set in the southeast direction. The hall cum dining is available in the northeast direction. The storeroom is placed near the kitchen is on the south side. Puja's room is kept on the south side. The Master bedroom is placed in the southwest direction with an attached toilet is in the west. Children's or kid's bedroom is available in the northwest direction. Common toilet is placed in the west inside of the house. portico is placed in the northeast outside of the home. Another Common toilet is available under the staircase is in the northwest direction. In this plan, you can keep a septic tank in the north or northwest direction near the staircase. Borewell or underground water tank you can place in the northeast direction.

On the First floor, The hall or living room is available in the northeast. The Home theatre room is placed in the south direction with an attached toilet is in the west. The bedroom is placed in the northwest direction with an attached toilet is in the west. The balcony is kept in the northeast. The staircase is placed outside of the house in the northwest direction. Pillars are marked in this house design plan is in the size 1'6"x9".

30X60 1800 SQFT NORTH FACING HOUSE PLAN

30x60 1800 sqft G+1 north-facing Home floor plan is given in this image. On the ground floor plan, the kitchen is provided in the southeast direction. Dining near the kitchen is in the east direction. Foyer is available near the dining. The Master bedroom is placed in the southwest direction with an attached toilet is in the west. Children's or kid's bedroom is available in the west direction with an attached toilet and the dressing room is in the northwest. The hall or living room is available in the northeast direction. Puja room is kept in the west. Sitout is placed in the northeast outside of the house. Portico or car parking is available in the north. The Septic tank is placed in the northwest direction. Borewell and the underground water tank are placed in the northeast direction.

On the First floor, The hall or living room is available in the northeast. The Master bedroom is placed in the southwest direction with an attached toilet with a shower room is in the southeast. . Children's or kid's bedroom is available in the west direction with an attached toilet and the dressing room is in the northwest. Home theatre is kept in the east direction. Common toilet is placed in the west. Foyer is available near the common toilet. The staircase is placed outside of the house in the northwest direction. Balcony is available in the northeast. Pillars are marked in this home design plan perfectly is in the size 1'6"x9".

36X50 1800 SQFT NORTH FACING HOUSE PLAN

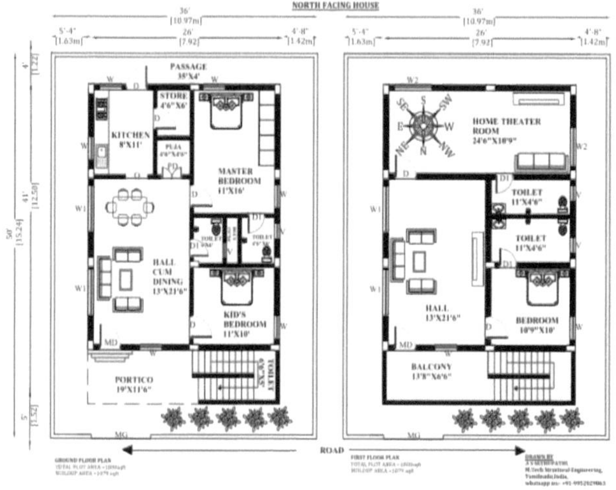

36x50 1800 sqft north-facing G+1 Home design floor plan is given in the above image. On the ground floor plan, the kitchen is provided in the southeast direction. The hall cum dining is available in the northeast direction. The storeroom is placed near the kitchen is in the south. Puja room is kept on the south side near the kitchen. The Master bedroom is placed in the southwest direction with an attached toilet is in the west. Children's or kid's bedroom is available in the northwest direction. Common toilet is placed in the west inside of the house. portico is placed in the northeast outside of the home. Another Common toilet is available under the staircase is in the northwest direction. In this plan, you can place the septic tank in the north or northwest direction near the staircase. Borewell or underground water tank you can place in the northeast direction.

On the First floor, The hall or living room is available in the northeast. The Home theatre room is placed in the south direction with an attached toilet is in the west. The bedroom is placed in the northwest direction with an attached toilet is in the west. The balcony is kept in the northeast. The staircase is placed outside of the house in the northwest direction. Pillars are marked in this house design plan perfectly is in the size 1'6"x9".

45X45 2025 SQFT NORTH FACING HOUSE PLAN

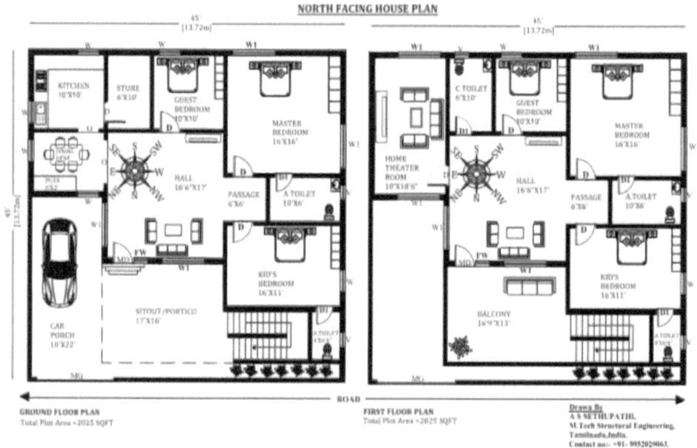

45x45 2025 sqft north-facing G+1 Home floor plan is given in the above image. On the ground floor plan, the kitchen is positioned in the southeast direction. Dining is placed near the kitchen is in the east. Puja room is kept inside the dining is on the east side. The storeroom is placed near the kitchen is in the south The hall is available in the northeast direction. The Master bedroom is placed in the southwest direction with an attached toilet is in the west. Children's or kid's bedroom is available in the northwest direction with an attached toilet is available is in the northwest backside of the stairs. . Guest bedroom is placed in the south. Sitout or the portico is placed in the northeast outside of the home. Carparking is placed in the east or the northeast. In this plan, you can keep the septic tank in the north or northwest direction near the staircase. Borewell or underground water tank you can place in the northeast direction.

On the First floor, The hall or living room is available in the northeast. The Home theatre room is placed in the southeast direction. The Master bedroom is placed in the southwest direction with an attached toilet is in the west. Children's or kid's bedroom is available in the northwest direction with an attached toilet is available is in the northwest. The guest bedroom is placed in the south and a common toilet is available near the guest bedroom is in the south direction. The balcony is kept in the northeast. The staircase is placed outside of the house in the northwest direction.

40X60 2400 SQFT NORTH FACING HOUSE PLAN

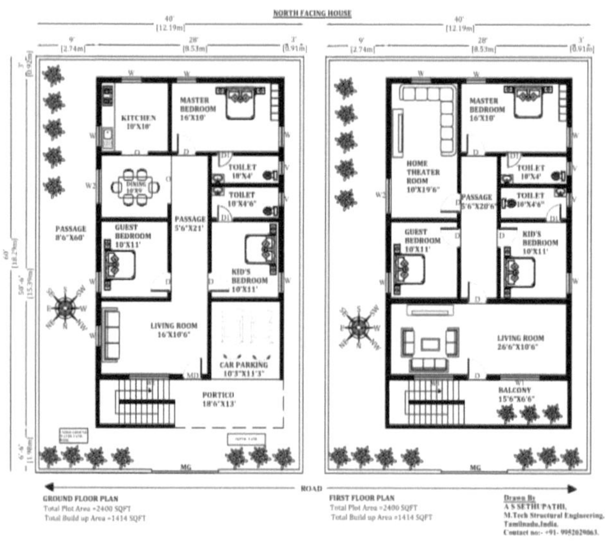

40x60 2400 sqft north-facing G+1 Home floor plan is given in the above image. On the ground floor plan, the kitchen is situated in the southeast direction. Dining is placed near the kitchen is in the east. The living room is available in the northeast direction. The Master bedroom is placed in the southwest direction with an attached toilet is in the west. Children's or kid's bedroom is available in the west with an attached toilet is available is in the west direction. The guest bedroom is placed in the east. The portico is placed in the northwest outside of the home. Carparking is available in the east of the northwest. The Septic tank is available in the northwest direction. Borewell and the underground water tank are placed in the northeast direction.

On the First floor, The hall or living room is available in the north. The Home theatre room is placed in the southeast direction. The Master bedroom is placed in the southwest direction with an attached toilet is in the west. Children's or kid's bedroom is available in the west direction with an attached toilet is available is in the west. The guest bedroom is placed in the east direction. The balcony is kept in the northwest. The staircase is placed outside of the house in the northeast direction.

60X40 2400 SQFT NORTH FACING HOUSE PLAN

60x40 2400 sqft north-facing G+1 House floor plan is given in the above image. On the ground floor plan, the kitchen is positioned in the southeast direction. Puja's room is kept on the west side. The hall is available in the northeast direction. The Master bedroom is placed in the southwest direction with an attached toilet is in the west. The study room is available in the west direction. The washroom and common toilet are available are in the northwest direction. The kid's bedroom is placed in the south. Passage or the portico is placed in the northeast outside of the house. The Garden area with Carparking is placed in the east. In this plan, you can place the septic tank in the north or northwest direction near the staircase. Borewell or underground water tank you can place in the northeast direction.

On the First floor, The living room is available in the northeast. The kitchen is placed in the southeast direction. The Master bedroom is placed in the southwest direction with an attached toilet and the dressing room is in the west. The guest bedroom is available in the south direction. Puja room is placed in the west. Utility and common toilet is placed in the northwest. Passage or Balcony is kept in the north. The staircase is placed outside of the house in the northwest direction.

SOUTH FACING HOUSE PLANS

22X22 484 SQFT SOUTH FACING HOUSE PLAN

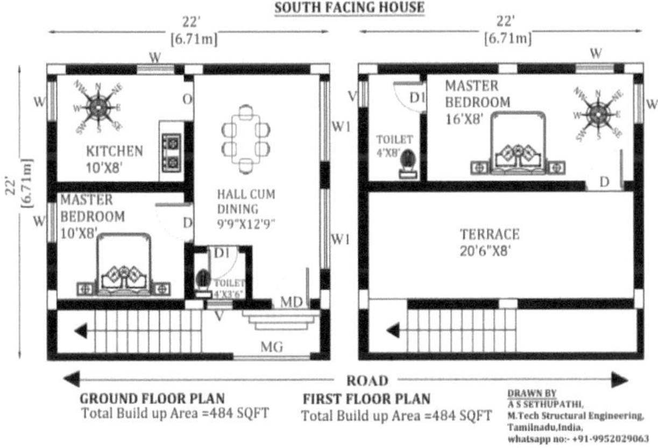

22x22 484 sqft south facing G+1 small House Plan is shown in the above image. On the ground floor plan, the kitchen is in the southeast direction. The Master Bedroom is placed in the southwest direction. Hall cum dining is in the Northeast direction. Common toilet is available in the south direction. On the First floor plan, the Master bedroom is in the northeast direction with an attached toilet is available in the northwest. The terrace is situated in the south. The staircase is available in the southwest direction outside of the house. Pillars are marked in this small home plan in the size of 1'6"x9".This home design plan is useful for people who searching for small floor plan ideas.

20X30 600 SQFT SOUTH FACING HOUSE PLAN

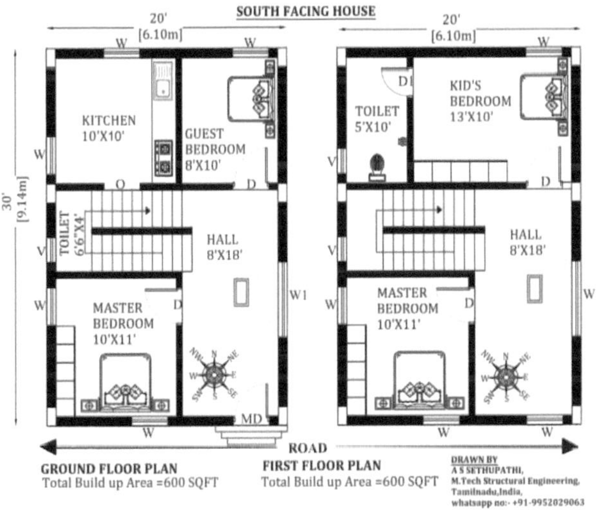

20x30 600 sqft G+1 south facing Home design plan is given in the above image. On the ground floor, the kitchen is set in the southeast direction. The Master bedroom is placed in the southwest direction. The guest bedroom is available in the northeast direction. The hall is available in the southeast direction. A common toilet is available under the stairs inside of the house.

On the First floor, The hall or living room is available in

the southeast. The Master bedroom is placed in the southwest direction. The kid's bedroom is placed in the northeast direction with an attached toilet is in the northwest. The staircase is placed inside of the house in the west direction. Pillars are mentioned in this home design plan are in the size 1'6"x9".

30X20 600 SQFT SOUTH FACING HOUSE PLAN

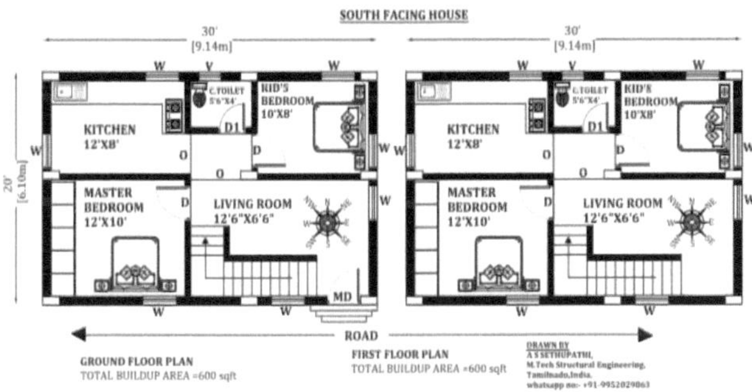

30x20 600 sqft G+1 south facing Home plan is given in the above image. On the ground floor, the kitchen is placed in the northwest direction. Placing the kitchen in the northwest direction is the second option as per vastu. The Master bedroom is placed in the southwest direction. The kid's bedroom is available in the northeast direction. Common toilet is placed in the north. The hall or Living room is available in the southeast direction.

The first-floor plan also the same as the ground floor plan. In that, the kitchen is placed in the northwest direction. The Master bedroom is placed in the southwest direction. The kid's bedroom is available in the northeast direction.

Common toilet is placed in the north. The hall or Living room is available in the southeast direction. The staircase is available inside of the house is in the south direction. The columns are marked in this home plan perfectly are in the size 1'6"x9".

25X25 625 SQFT SOUTH FACING HOUSE PLAN

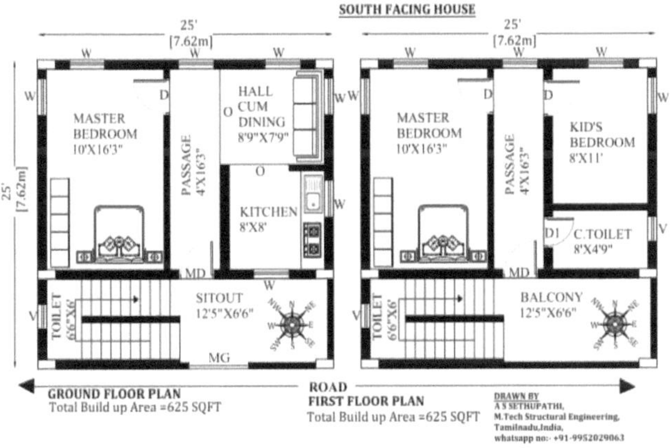

25x25 625 sqft south facing G+1 Home design plan is given in the above image. On the ground floor plan, the kitchen is provided in the southeast direction. The Master bedroom is placed in the west direction. The hall cum Dining is available in the northeast direction. The passage is available in the center of the house. Common toilet is available under the stairs outside of the house is in the southwest. Sitout is placed in the southeast direction.

On the First floor, The Master bedroom is placed in the

west direction. The kid's bedroom is placed in the northeast direction. The common toilet is in the southeast. The passage is available in the center. The staircase is placed outside of the house in the southwest direction. Pillars are mentioned in this house design plan are in the size 1'6"x9".

26X26 676 SQFT SOUTH FACING HOUSE PLAN

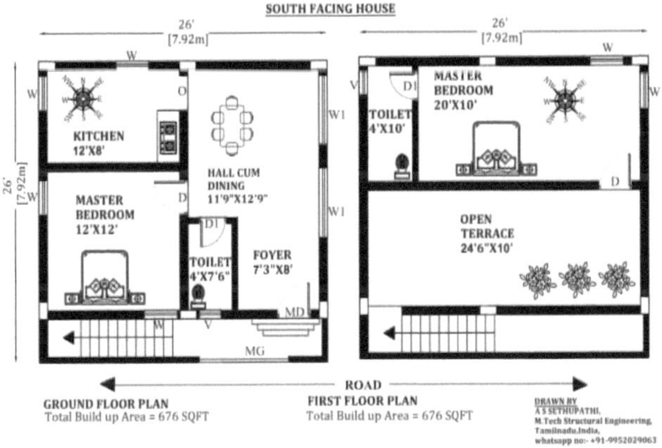

26x26 676 sqft G+1 south facing Home design plan is given in the above image. On the ground floor, the kitchen is set in the northwest direction. The hall cum dining is available in the northeast direction. The Master bedroom is placed in the southwest direction. A common toilet is available in the south near the master bedroom. The foyer is in the southeast corner of the home.

On the First floor, The Open terrace is available in the south. The Master bedroom is placed in the northeast direction with an attached toilet is in the northwest. The staircase is placed outside of the house in the southwest direction. Pillars are mentioned in this home design are in the size 1'6"x9".

20X40 800 SQFT SOUTH FACING HOUSE PLAN

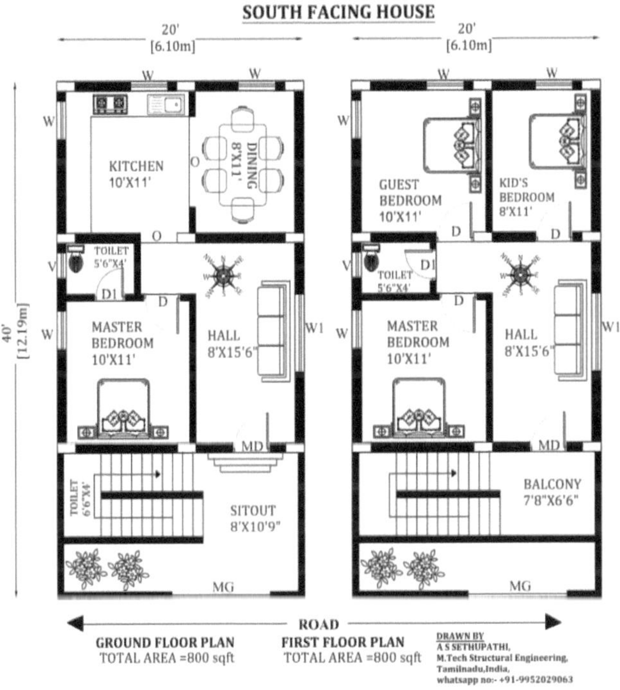

20x40 800 sqft G+1 South facing House design plan is given in the above image. On the ground floor, the kitchen is placed in the northwest direction. The dining room is placed near the kitchen is in the northeast. The Master bedroom is placed in the southwest direction with an attached toilet is in the west. The hall or living room is available in the southeast direction. Sitout is placed in the southeast outside of the house. A common toilet is available under the staircase is in the southwest direction.

On the First floor plan, The hall or living room is available in the southeast. The Master bedroom is provided in the southwest direction. The kid's bedroom is positioned in the northeast direction. The guest bedroom is available in the northwest. Common toilet is placed in the west. The staircase is placed outside of the house in the southwest direction. The balcony is available in the southeast direction. Pillars are marked in this home design are in the size 1'6"x9". Room dimensions are given clearly in this plan.

22X40 880 SQFT SOUTH FACING HOUSE PLAN

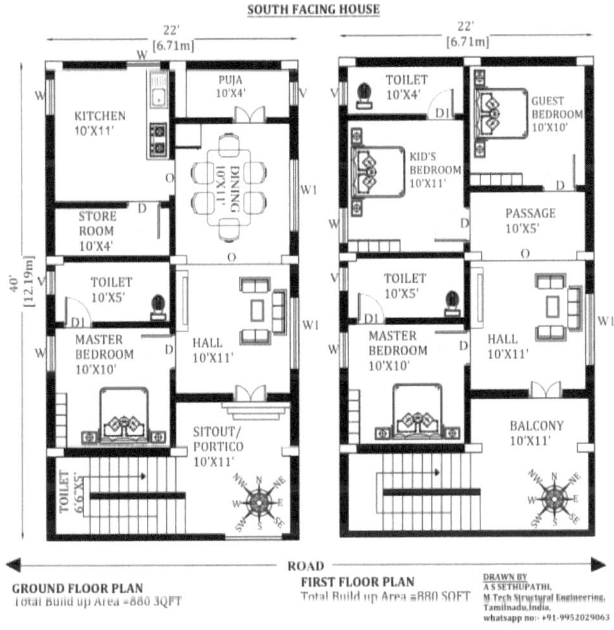

22x40 880 sqft South facing G+1 House design plan is given in the above image. On the ground floor, the kitchen is set in the northwest direction. The dining room is placed near the kitchen is in the east. The storeroom is available in the west near the kitchen. Puja room is positioned in the

18x50 900 sqft South facing G+1 House design plan is given in the above image. On the ground floor, the kitchen is situated in the southeast direction. The dining room is placed near the kitchen is in the east. Puja room is placed in the southwest. The Master bedroom is placed in the north direction with an attached toilet is in the west. The kid's bedroom is placed in the west. The hall or living room is available in the west direction. Sitout or the portico is placed in the southwest outside of the house. A common toilet is available under the staircase is in the southeast direction.

On the First floor plan, the kitchen is placed in the southeast direction. The dining room is placed near the kitchen is in the east. Puja room is placed in the southwest. The Master bedroom is placed in the north direction with an attached toilet is in the west. The kid's bedroom is placed in the west. The hall or living room is available in the west direction. The balcony is placed in the southwest outside of the house. Common toilet is in the east direction.

30X30 900 SQFT SOUTH FACING HOUSE PLAN

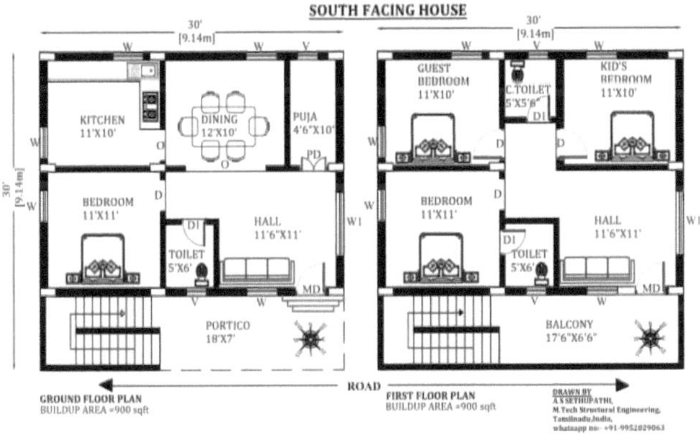

30x30 900 sqft South facing G+1 House design plan is given in the above image. On the ground floor, the kitchen is placed in the northwest direction. The dining room is placed near the kitchen is in the north. Puja room is placed near the dining is in the northeast. The Master bedroom is placed in the southwest direction. Common toilet is available in the south direction. The hall or living room is available in the southeast direction. Portico is placed in the southeast outside of the house.

On the First floor plan, The hall or living room is available in the southeast. The Master bedroom is placed in the southwest direction with an attached toilet is in the south. The kid's bedroom is placed in the northeast direction. A guest bedroom is situated in the northwest. Common toilet is available in the north direction. The staircase is placed outside of the house in the southwest direction. A balcony is available in the southeast direction. Pillars are mentioned clearly in this home design is in the size 1'6"x9". Room dimensions are given perfectly in this plan.

26X36 936 SQFT SOUTH FACING HOUSE PLAN

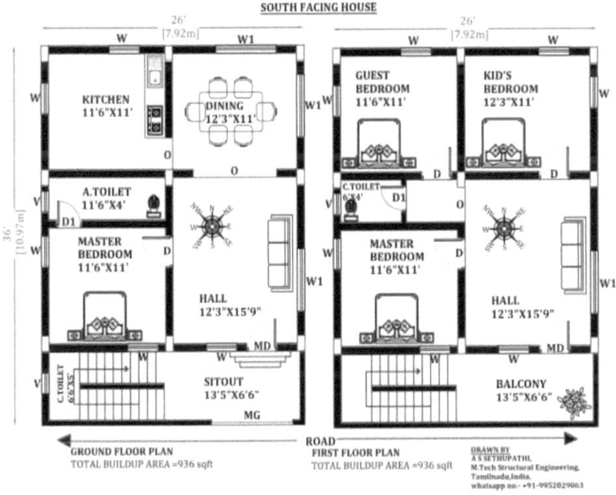

26x36 936 sqft South facing G+1 House design plan is given in the above image. On the ground floor, the kitchen is set in the northwest direction. The dining room is placed near the kitchen is in the northeast. The Master bedroom is placed in the southwest direction with an attached toilet is in the west. Common toilet is available in the southwest direction under the stairs. The hall or living room is available in the southeast direction. Portico or sitout is placed in the southeast outside of the house.

On the First floor plan, The hall or living room is available in the southeast. The Master bedroom is placed in the southwest direction. The kid's bedroom is placed in the northeast direction. The guest bedroom is available in the northwest. Common toilet is available in the west direction. The staircase is placed outside of the house in the southwest direction. A balcony is available in the southeast direction. Pillars are mentioned clearly in this house design is in the size 1'6"x9". Room dimensions are given perfectly in this plan.

36X26 936 SQFT SOUTH FACING HOUSE PLAN

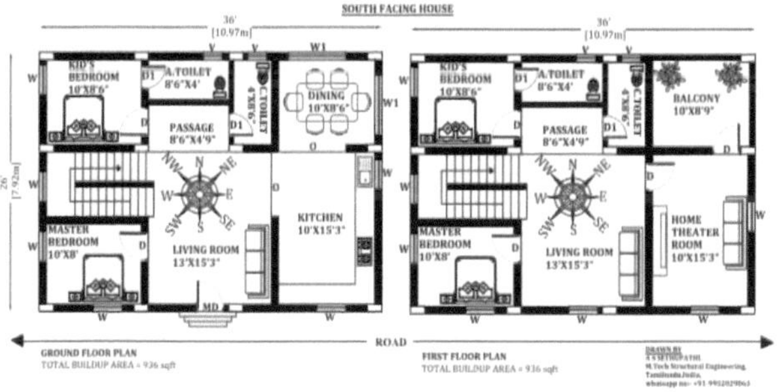

36x26 936 sqft G+1 South facing Home design plan is given in the above image. On the ground floor, the kitchen is positioned in the southeast direction. The dining room is placed near the kitchen is in the northeast. The Master bedroom is placed in the southwest direction. The kid's bedroom is in the northwest with an attached toilet is in the north. Common toilet is available in the north direction. The hall or living room is available in the south direction.

On the First floor plan, The hall or living room is available in the south. The Master bedroom is placed in the southwest direction. The kid's bedroom is placed in the northwest direction with an attached toilet is in the north. The Home theatre room is available in the southeast. Common toilet is available in the north direction. The staircase is placed inside of the house in the west direction. The balcony is available in the northeast direction. Pillars are mentioned clearly in this house design is in the size 1'6"x9".Perfect Room dimensions are given in this plan.

24X40 960 SQFT SOUTH FACING HOUSE PLAN

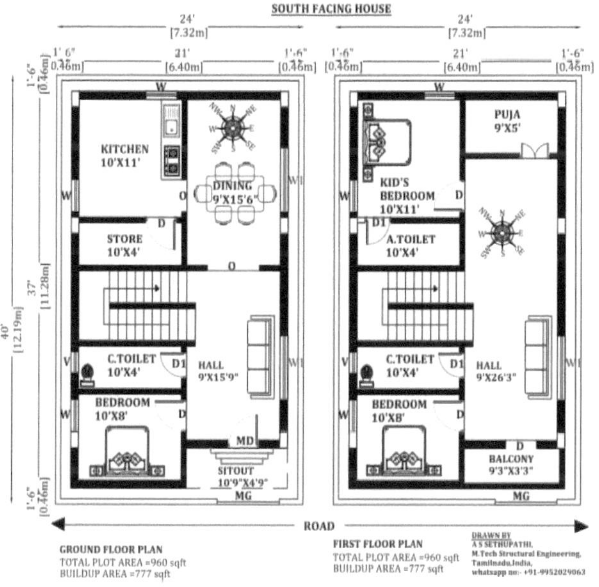

24x40 960 sqft G+1 South facing Home design plan is given in the above image. On the ground floor, the kitchen is situated in the southeast direction. The dining room is placed near the kitchen is in the northeast. The storeroom is placed in the west near the kitchen. The Master bedroom is placed in the southwest direction. Common toilet is available in the west direction. The hall or living room is available in the southeast direction.

On the First floor plan, The hall or living room is available in the southeast. The Master bedroom is placed in the southwest direction. The kid's bedroom is placed in the northwest direction with an attached toilet is in the west. Puja room is available in the northeast. Common toilet is available in the west direction. The staircase is placed inside of the house in the west direction. The balcony is available in the southeast direction. Pillars are mentioned clearly in this house design is in the size 1'6"x9".Perfect Room dimensions are given in this plan.

26X40 1040 SQFT SOUTH FACING HOUSE PLAN

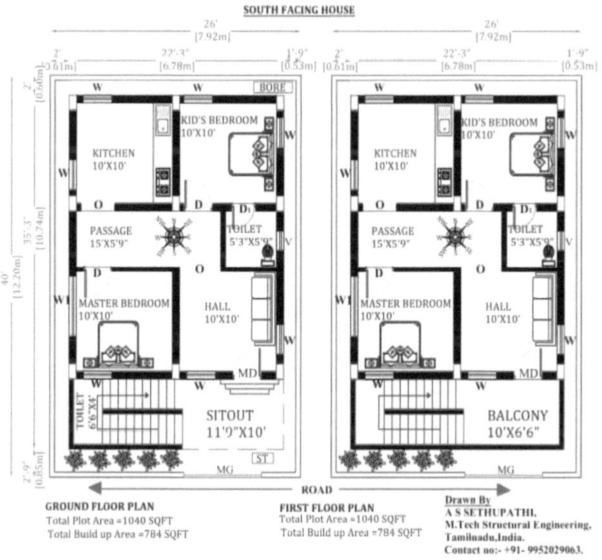

26x40 1040 sqft G+1 south facing Home plan design is given in the above image. On the ground floor plan, the kitchen is set in the northwest direction. The Master bedroom is placed in the southwest direction. The kid's bedroom is available in the northeast direction with an attached toilet is in the east. Common toilet is placed under the stairs is in the southwest. The hall or Living room is available in the southeast direction. The sitout is placed in the southeast direction outside of the house.

The first-floor plan also the same as the ground floor plan. In that, the kitchen is placed in the northwest direction. The Master bedroom is provided in the southwest direction. The kid's bedroom is available in the northeast direction with an attached toilet is in the east. The hall or Living room is available in the southeast direction. The balcony is placed in the southeast direction outside of the home.A staircase is available outside of the house is in the southwest direction. The columns are marked in this house plan perfectly are in the size 1'6"x9".

33X33 1089 SQFT SOUTH FACING HOUSE PLAN

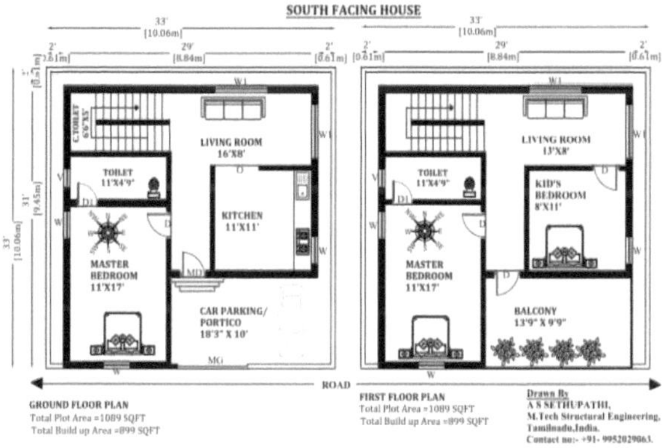

33x33 1089 sqft south facing G+1 Home plan design is given in the above image. On the ground floor plan, the kitchen is set in the southeast direction. The Master bedroom is placed in the southwest direction with an attached toilet is in the west. Common toilet is placed under the stairs is in the northwest. The hall or Living room is available in the northeast direction. The car parking or the portico is placed in the southeast direction outside of the house.

On the first floor plan, The Master bedroom is placed in

the southwest direction with an attached toilet is in the west. The kid's bedroom is available in the east direction. The hall or Living room is available in the northeast direction. The balcony is placed in the southeast direction outside of the home. Staircase is available inside of the house is in the northwest direction.

23X50 1150 SQFT SOUTH FACING HOUSE PLAN

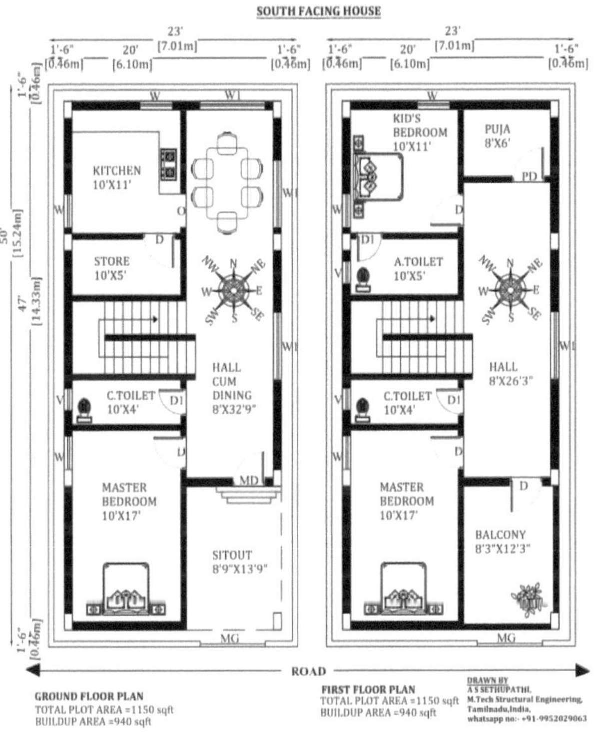

23x50 1150 sqft G+1 South facing Home design plan is given in the above image. On the ground floor, the kitchen is placed in the northwest direction. Hall cum Dining

Room is placed in the east. The storeroom is placed in the west near the kitchen. The Master bedroom is placed in the southwest direction. Common toilet is available in the west direction. Sitout is placed in the southeast direction outside of the house.

On the First floor plan, The hall or living room is available in the east. The Master bedroom is placed in the southwest direction. The kid's bedroom is positioned in the northwest direction with an attached toilet is in the west. Puja room is available in the northeast. Common toilet is available in the west direction. The staircase is placed inside of the house in the west direction. A balcony is available in the southeast direction. The pillars are mentioned in this house design are in the size 1'6"x9".Perfect Room dimensions are given in this home plan.

20X60 1200 SQFT SOUTH FACING HOUSE PLAN

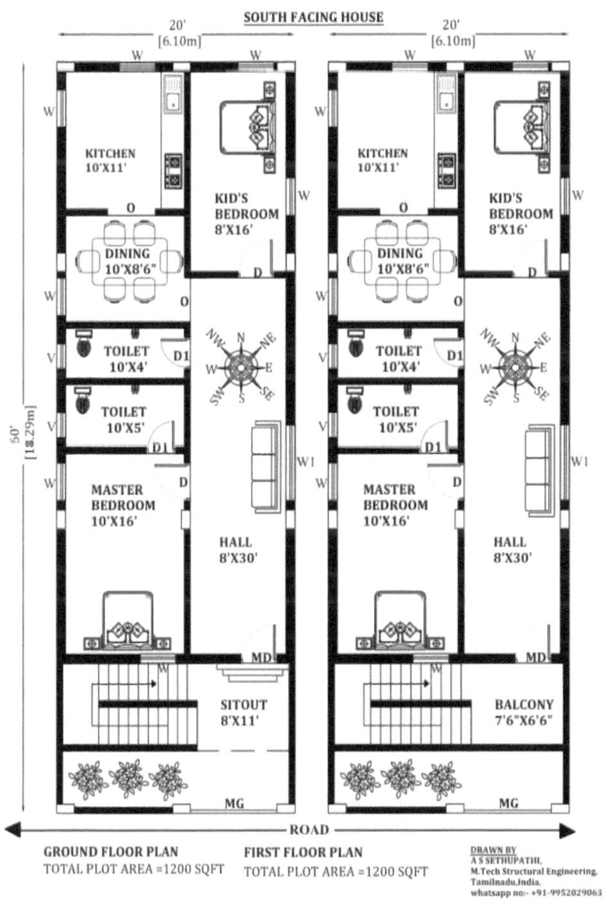

20x60 1200 sqft G+1 south facing Home plan design is given in the above image. On the ground floor plan, the kitchen is situated in the northwest direction. Dining is placed near the kitchen is in the west. The Master bedroom is placed in the southwest direction with an attached toilet is in the west. The kid's bedroom is available in the northeast. Common toilet is placed in the west. The hall or Living room is available in the southeast direction. The sitout is placed in the southeast direction outside of the house.

The first-floor plan also the same as a ground-floor plan. In that, the kitchen is placed in the northwest direction. Dining is placed near the kitchen is in the west. The Master bedroom is placed in the southwest direction with an attached toilet is in the west. The kid's bedroom is available in the northeast. Common toilet is placed in the west. The hall or Living room is available in the southeast direction. The balcony is placed in the southeast direction outside of the home. Staircase is available outside of the house is in the southwest direction. The columns are marked in this house plan perfectly are in the size 1'6"x9". Room dimensions are mentioned in this plan.

30X40 1200 SQFT SOUTH FACING HOUSE PLAN

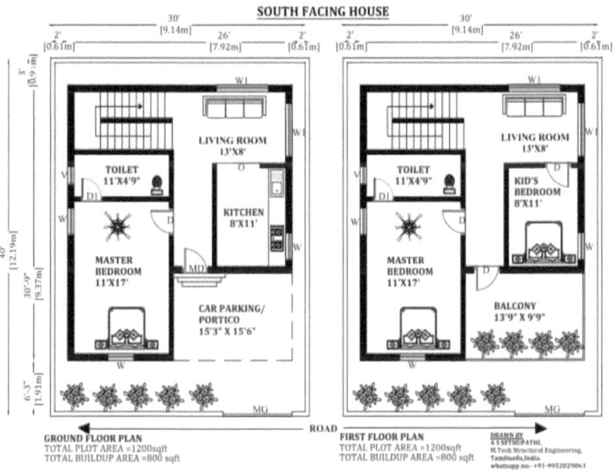

30 x 40 1200 sqft south facing G+1 Home plan design is given in the above image. On the ground floor plan, the kitchen is set in the southeast direction. The Master bedroom is placed in the southwest direction with an attached toilet is in the west. The hall or Living room is available in the northeast direction. The car parking or the portico is placed in the southeast direction outside of the house.

On the first floor plan, The Master bedroom is placed in the southwest direction with an attached toilet is in the west. The kid's bedroom is available in the east direction. The hall or Living room is available in the northeast direction. The balcony is placed in the southeast direction outside of the home. Staircase is available inside of the house is in the northwest direction.

40X30 1200 SQFT SOUTH FACING HOUSE PLAN

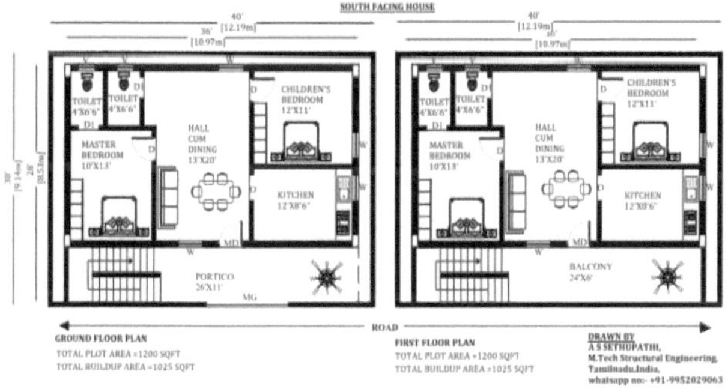

40 x 30 1200 sqft south facing G+1 House plan design is given in the above image. On the ground floor plan, the kitchen is situated in the southeast direction. The hall cum dining is available in the center of the house. The Master bedroom is placed in the southwest direction with an attached toilet is in the northwest. The children's bedroom is available in the northeast direction of the house. Common toilet is available in the north. The portico is placed in the southeast direction outside of the house.

The first-floor plan also the same as the ground floor plan. In that, the kitchen is placed in the southeast direction. The hall cum dining is available in the center of the house.

The Master bedroom is placed in the southwest direction with an attached toilet is in the northwest. The children's bedroom is available in the northeast direction of the house. Common toilet is available in the north. The balcony is placed in the southeast direction outside of the home. Staircase is available outside of the house is in the southwest direction. The columns are mentioned in this house plan perfectly are in the size 1'6"x9".

25X50 1250 SQFT SOUTH FACING HOUSE PLAN

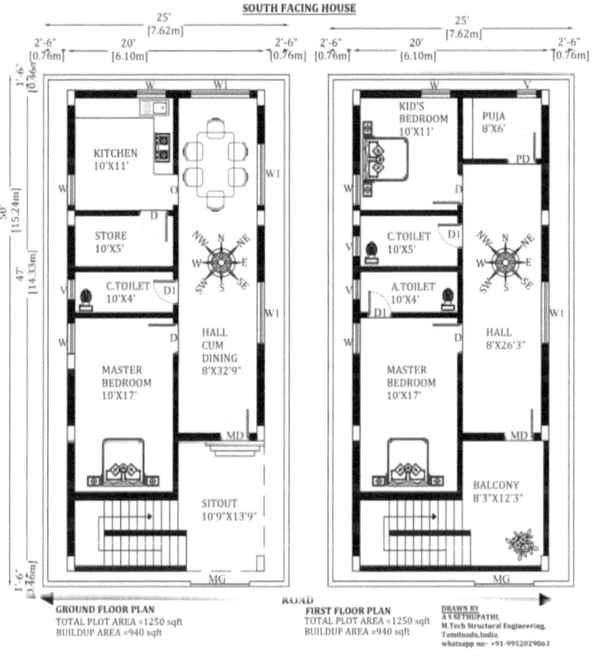

25x50 1250 sqft South facing G+1 Home design plan is given in the above image. On the ground floor, the kitchen is provided in the northwest direction. Hall cum Dining Room is placed in the east. The storeroom is placed in the west near the kitchen. The Master bedroom is placed in the southwest direction. Common toilet is available in the west direction. Sitout is placed in the southeast direction outside of the house.

On the First floor plan, The hall or living room is available in the east. The Master bedroom is placed in the southwest direction with an attached toilet is in the west. The kid's bedroom is placed in the northwest direction. Puja room is available in the northeast. Common toilet is available in the west direction. The staircase is placed outside of the house in the southwest direction. The balcony is available in the southeast direction. The pillars are mentioned in this house design are in the size 1'6"x9".Perfect Room dimensions are given in this house floor plan.

27X50 1350 SQFT SOUTH FACING HOUSE PLAN

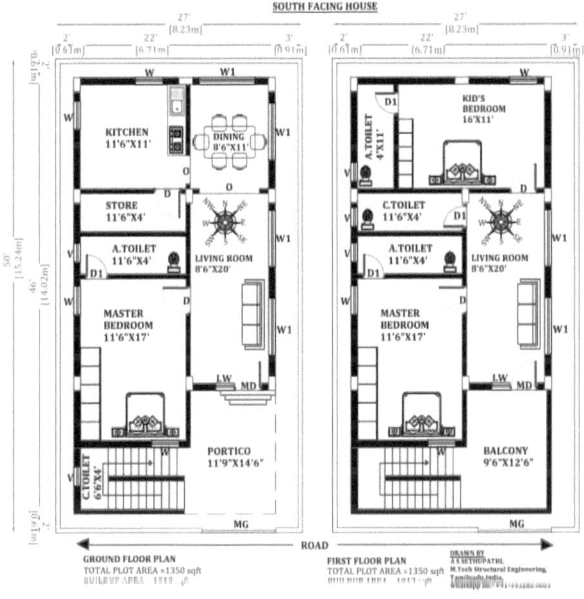

27x50 1350 sqft South facing G+1 House design plan is given in the above image. On the ground floor, the kitchen is set in the northwest direction. The dining room is in the northeast. The living room is placed in the southeast. The storeroom is placed near the kitchen is in the west. The

Master bedroom is placed in the southwest direction with an attached toilet is in the west. Portico is placed in the southeast direction outside of the house.

On the First floor plan, The hall or living room is available in the southeast. The Master bedroom is placed in the southwest direction with an attached toilet is in the west. The kid's bedroom is placed in the northeast direction with an attached toilet is in the southwest. Common toilet is available in the west direction. The staircase is placed outside of the house in the southwest direction. A balcony is available in the southeast direction. The pillars are mentioned in this house design are in the size 1'6"x9".Perfect Room dimensions are given in this house floor plan.

35X40 1400 SQFT SOUTH FACING HOUSE PLAN

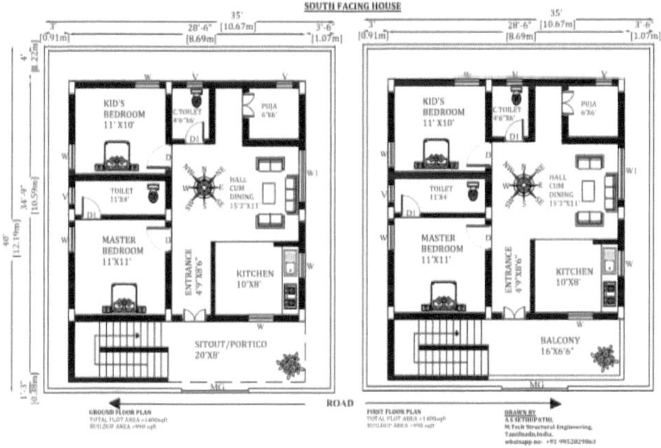

35x40 1400 sqft South facing G+1 Home floor plan is given in the above image. On the ground floor, the kitchen is positioned in the southeast direction. Hall cum Dining Room is placed in the east. Puja room is placed in the northeast. The Master bedroom is placed in the southwest direction with an attached toilet is in the west. The kid's bedroom is placed in the northwest direction. Common toilet is available in the north direction. Sitout or the portico is placed in the southeast direction outside of the house.

The first-floor plan is also the same as the Ground floor plan. In that, the kitchen is placed in the southeast direction. Hall cum Dining Room is placed in the east. Puja room is placed in the northeast. The Master bedroom is placed in the southwest direction with an attached toilet is in the west. The kid's bedroom is placed in the northwest direction. Common toilet is available in the north direction. The staircase is placed outside of the house in the southwest direction. A balcony is available in the southeast direction. Pillars are marked in this home design are in the size 1'6"x9".Perfect Room dimensions are given in this house floor plan.

30X50 1500 SQFT SOUTH FACING HOUSE PLAN

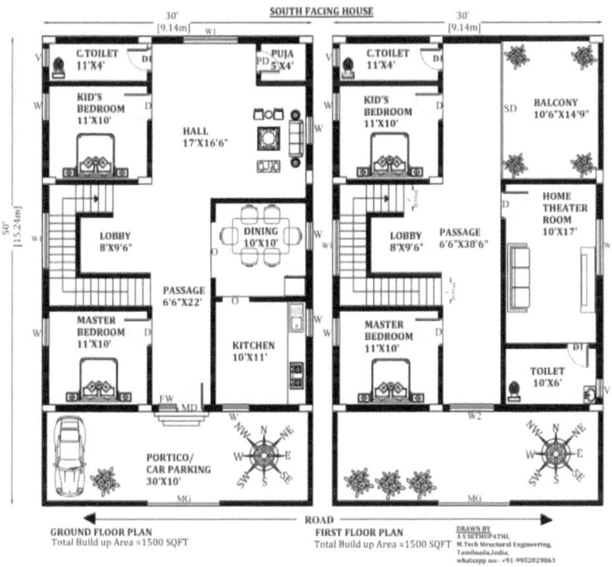

30x50 1500 sqft G+1 South facing Home floor plan is given in the above image. On the ground floor, the kitchen is situated in the southeast direction. The dining room is placed near the kitchen is in the east. The Master bedroom is placed in the southwest direction. The kid's bedroom is in the west. Common toilet is available in the northwest direction. The hall or living room is available in the east direction. Lobby and Passage are available. Puja room is kept in the northeast.

On the First floor plan, The Balcony is available in the northeast. The Master bedroom is placed in the southwest direction. The kid's bedroom is in the west. Common toilet is available in the northwest direction. A Home theatre room is available in the east with an attached toilet is in the southeast. The staircase is placed inside of the house in the west direction. Pillars are mentioned clearly in this house design is in the size 1'6"x9". Room dimensions are given in this plan Perfectly.

30X60 1800 SQFT SOUTH FACING HOUSE PLAN

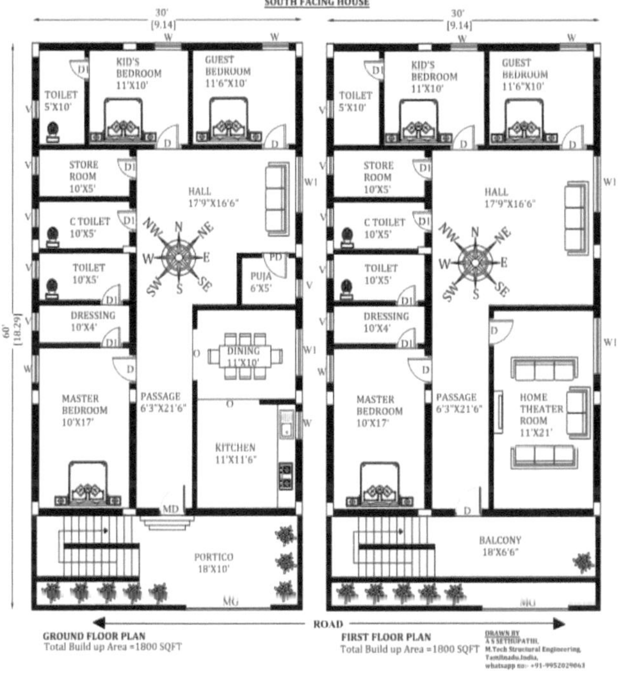

30x60 1800 sqft G+1 South facing House floor plan is given in the above image. On the ground floor plan, the kitchen is placed in the southeast direction. The dining room is placed near the kitchen is in the east. The storeroom is placed in the west. Puja room is kept in the east direction near the dining. The Master bedroom is placed in the southwest direction with an attached dressing room and the toilet is in the west. The kid's bedroom is in the north with an attached toilet is placed in the northwest. A guest bedroom is placed in the northeast direction. Common toilet is available in the west direction. The hall or living room is available in the east direction.

On the First floor plan, The Balcony is available in the southeast. The Master bedroom is provided in the southwest direction with an attached dressing room and the toilet is in the west. The kid's bedroom is in the north with an attached toilet is placed in the northwest. A guest bedroom is placed in the northeast direction. Common toilet is available in the west direction. The storeroom is placed in the west direction. The Home theatre room is available in the southeast. The staircase is placed outside of the house in the southwest direction. Pillars are mentioned clearly in this house design is in the size 1'6"x9". Room dimensions are given in this plan neatly.

36X50 1800 SQFT SOUTH FACING HOUSE PLAN

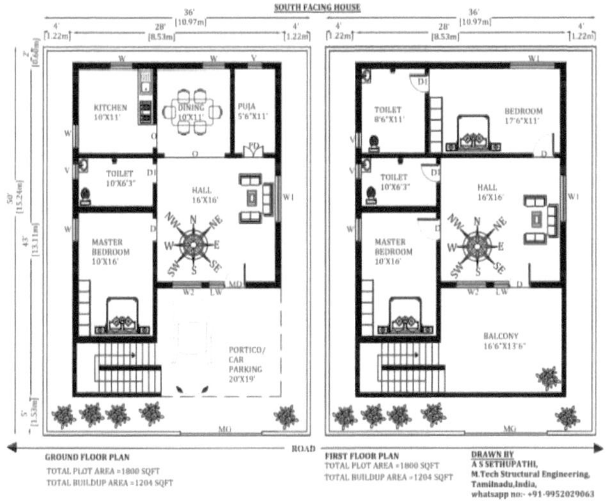

36x50 1800 sqft South facing G+1 House design plan is given in the above image. On the ground floor, the kitchen is set in the northwest direction. The dining room is in the north. Puja room is kept in the northeast direction. The living room or the hall is provided in the east. The Master bedroom is placed in the southwest direction. The common toilet is in the west direction. A portico or car parking is placed in the southeast direction outside of the house.

On the First floor plan, The hall or living room is available in the east. The Master bedroom is situated in the southwest direction. The kid's bedroom is placed in the northeast direction with an attached toilet is in the northwest. Common toilet is available in the west direction. The staircase is placed outside of the house in the southwest direction. A balcony is available in the southeast direction. Room dimensions are given neatly in this house floor plan.

45X45 2025 SQFT SOUTH FACING HOUSE PLAN

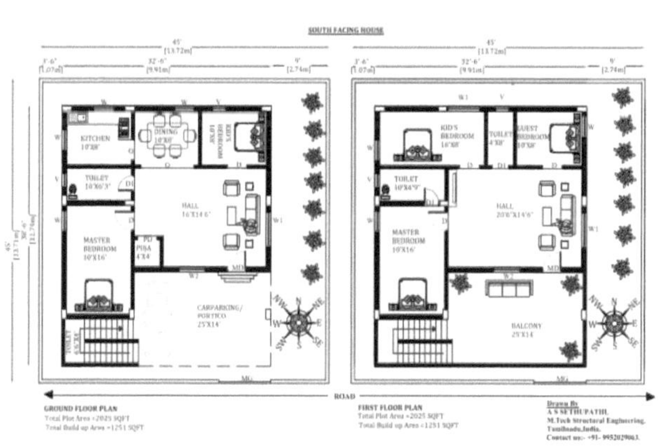

45x45 2025 sqft South facing G+1 House design plan is given in the above image. On the ground floor plan, the kitchen is placed in the northwest direction. The dining room is in the north. Puja room is kept in the south direction. The living room or the hall is set in the east. The Master bedroom is placed in the southwest direction. The kid's bedroom is placed in the northeast. Common toilet is placed in the west. And another common toilet is available in the southwest direction under the stairs outside. A portico or car parking is placed in the southeast direction outside of the house.

On the First floor plan, The hall or living room is available in the east. The Master bedroom is positioned in the southwest direction with an attached toilet is placed in the west direction. The kid's bedroom is placed in the northwest direction. The Guest bedroom is in the northeast. Common toilet is available in the north direction. The staircase is placed outside of the house in the southwest direction. The balcony is available in the southeast direction. Room dimensions are given neatly in this house floor plan. Pillars are marked clearly in this house design is in the size 1'6"x9". Furniture details are given neatly in this plan.

40X60 2400 SQFT SOUTH FACING HOUSE PLAN

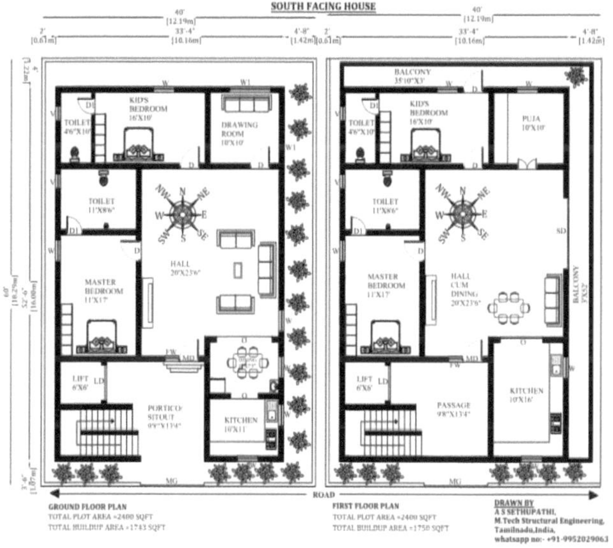

40x60 2400 sqft South facing G+1 Houe floor plan is given in the above image. On the ground floor, the kitchen is placed in the southeast direction. Dining near the kitchen is in the east. Hall placed in the east direction. The drawing room is situated in the northeast. The Master bedroom is placed in the southwest direction with an attached toilet is in the west. The kid's bedroom is placed in the north direction with an attached toilet is in the northwest. Sitout or the portico is placed in the southeast direction outside of the house.

On the First floor plan, the kitchen is placed in the southeast direction. Hall cum Dining Room is placed in the east. Pooja room is placed in the northeast. The Master bedroom is placed in the southwest direction with an attached toilet is in the west. The kid's bedroom is placed in the north direction with an attached toilet is in the northwest. The Lift is placed in the west near the stairs outside. a staircase is placed in the southwest direction outside of the house. A balcony is available in the north and the east direction. Perfect Room dimensions are given in this house floor plan. Furniture are set perfectly in this home plan.

60X40 2400 SQFT SOUTH FACING HOUSE PLAN

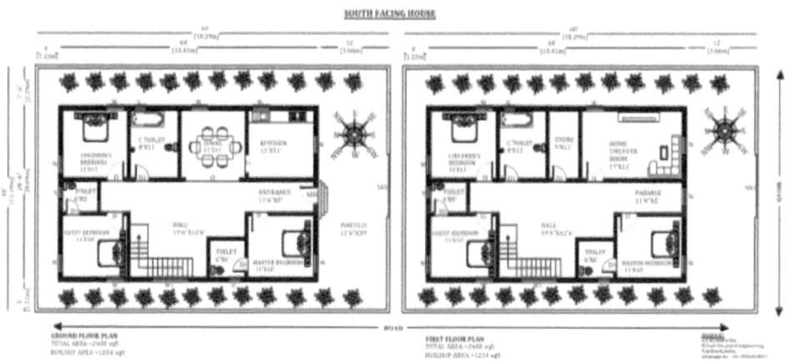

60x40 2400 sqft G+1 South facing Home floor plan is given in the above image. On the ground floor plan, the kitchen is placed in the southeast direction. The dining room is placed near the kitchen is in the east. The Master bedroom is positioned in the southwest direction with an attached toilet is in the west. The children's bedroom is placed in the northeast. A guest bedroom is kept in the northwest with an attached toilet is in the north. Common toilet is available in the east direction. The hall or living room is available in the west direction. Portico is available in the south outside of the house.

On the First floor plan, The Master bedroom is placed in the southwest direction with an attached toilet is in the west. Kid's or children's bedroom is in the northeast. A guest bedroom is kept in the northwest with an attached toilet is in the north. Common toilet is available in the east direction. The storeroom is placed near the home theatre room is in the east. The Home theatre room is available in the southeast. The staircase is placed inside of the house in the west direction. Room dimensions are given in this home plan Perfectly.

www.ingramcontent.com/pod-product-compliance
Ingram Content Group UK Ltd.
Pitfield, Milton Keynes, MK11 3LW, UK
UKHW041954190726
13854UKWH00005B/1963